Go 4 It!

Start Getting What You Want in Your
Finances, Career, Health & Relationships
(because YES you really *can* have it all!)

ROBERT PASCUZZI

ISBN # 9781793817372

CONTENTS

FOREWORD

When I first met Bob Pascuzzi in the early 2000s, he was one of the top insurance agents in the city. He wanted to make sure his clients had estate plans in place, and he reached out to me to help put those documents together for his clients. I got to see Bob in action and, while he was easily one of the top performers I'd ever known, it was clear he wasn't very happy. As my career progressed, I moved into more comprehensive wealth management business and started providing financial planning, money management, and legal work to clients through Creative Planning. Bob and I stayed in touch and I continued to work with his clients.

I was always fascinated when I spent time with Bob; he was always listening to self-help tapes, reading self-help books, and telling me what he had learned.

It wasn't uncommon to come into the office first thing in the morning and hear an inspiring message from Bob on my phone – something he might have listened to while working out, long before I had woken up.

One morning, I came to work and Bob was sitting in a cubicle outside my office. I asked Bob what he was doing here and he explained he had been listening to some tapes and the tapes had encouraged him to pursue his dreams and that success would follow. I asked him exactly what his dreams were, and he said he really wanted to start doing the right thing for the client all the time, rather than selling a product for the company he worked for. As a financial adviser, I quickly suggested that perhaps it was not the greatest idea for Bob to leave his very high income behind and start over from scratch. He assured me that he had thought it through that morning and that's what he was going to do.

The next day I came out of my office, and there was Bob again, and it occurred to me that he was really here to stay. It wasn't long before Bob and I started working on 401K plans, which we found a very rewarding experience. We were able to help businesses and, more important, all the participants in the 401K plan, greatly reduce their cost, improve their investments options, and also give them the opportunity to work with a fiduciary, someone who would work in their best interests.

Today Creative Planning manages approximately $33 billion in assets and the 401K business has had an enormous impact under Bob's leadership. But this is not what most impresses me about Bob: I have never in my entire life met anyone so dedicated and intentional about being the absolute best person he can be and investing his time in making sure he is doing everything he can to be the best husband, father, adviser and friend. While I gained a great colleague, what's more significant to me is that I consider Bob one of the best friends I've ever had; he's really more like a brother.

Whatever it is Bob has been learning over the years, it certainly worked for him and it has impacted those around him, who can't help but be inspired by his commitment to self-improvement and realizing his best self. I have had the benefit of spending hundreds of hours with Bob, and the experience has changed my life. This book is the next-best thing to spending time with Bob. I am sure the time you dedicate to reading it will reap countless rewards for you.

— Peter Mallouk, JD, MBA, CFP
President and Chief Investment Officer of Creative Planning and affiliated companies

INTRODUCTION

Only those who attempt the absurd can
achieve the impossible.
Albert Einstein

I'm truly grateful to you for choosing this book and hope you are ready to strap yourself in for an exciting ride that is intended to bring nothing less than radical change to your life. Wherever you are on life's journey, I'm certain you have dreams that are unfulfilled. This is the roadmap that will lead you to your destiny.

You're probably familiar with the term "go for it." It means leaping into action when all other options have expired and one has nothing left to lose. It's that moment in the movies when the hero, in a last-ditch effort to save humanity, aims his rocket at the asteroid hurtling toward Earth. And it can also refer to a time in your life when you finally take a good, hard look at things and decide it's time for a change.

My *Go 4 It!* program will allow you to see your life as the singular grand adventure it is, and to recognize that today is the day you must take a stand.

It is far better to be courageous and take action than it is to sit idly by and let circumstances (and other people) dictate the story of your life. You will discover the truth in this paradox: It is better to love failure than to fear it, and failure is the quickest path to success.

I have studied successful people and invariably the "naturals" talk about how they cherish their mistakes because the lessons learned served them well and sculpted them into the people they became. They almost always possess an innate fearlessness and conviction that they will find the solution to whatever problems may arise. They seem to instinctively know that we will always find opportunity in challenges.

I did not start out as a successful person. And, for those of us who were not born with the "go-for-it" gene, I've observed that those of us who don't consider ourselves innately successful have a logical explanation for why they we stood still at crucial times when opportunity came knocking. We will say things like: the "time wasn't right," or "my friends (or wife or husband), discouraged me," or we weren't "certain" we would succeed at whatever it was we knew we needed to do.

The desire to avoid failure at all costs and hide in the middle of the herd is the conventional wisdom most of us have been taught since childhood. We desperately crave safety and security. Once we are tossed out from the protective cloak of Mom and Dad, we soon discover that the real world can be ruthless. Despite this reality, the vast majority of the population will continue to seek security and be lulled into lives of underachievement and mediocrity.

But this book is not for the vast majority.

It is for those of us who are ready to make the decision to live with intention and take full advantage of the precious time we have on this planet.

Because I'm not one of those natural-born "go-for-it" people, I've studied and applied trial-and-error techniques through the years to transform my life.

And now, with a sense of humility and gratitude, I would like to share my knowledge with you.

In my case, my belief system told me that if I followed the rules, I would eventually be safe and secure and that the sensible thing was to settle for a "good enough" life. However, when I had my awakening, I was forced to come face-to-face with the uncomfortable reality that this approach would cause me to miss out on the incredible life that is ours for the taking, and that I was ultimately condemning myself to a lifetime of regret.

If you can relate to this, and feel a fire in your belly, then you are ripe to join the *Go 4 It!* movement.

There is a moment of truth in the movie *Home Alone*, when eight-year-old Kevin McCallister (played by Macaulay Culkin) realizes that the time has finally arrived when he must launch his attack on the two hapless criminals he has lured into his elaborately booby-trapped home. He locks and loads his air-rifle, then calmly steels himself with these simple words:

"This is it! … don't get scared now."

And then, in one of the most hilarious episodes of slapstick comedy ever filmed, he proceeds to take Marv and Harry down.

Introduction

I'll often turn to a colleague and repeat Kevin's words as we're about to leap into a challenging situation, and it always induces a knowing laugh. But it's not just the famous phrase that fits with the *Go 4 It!* Philosophy – it's also the fact that Kevin identified his enemies and prepared extensively to defeat them. This book will help you identify the enemy (largely – and surprisingly, possibly – you're going to discover that the biggest enemy resides in your head).

Come armed with a highlighter, a pen and a notebook because we've got some work to do. I've written *Go 4 It!* so that you can read it in an afternoon. My goal is nothing less than to set you on your path to a new life by the time you turn the last page.

So, power down your phone (or actually leave the house without it – what a concept!), find a nice, quiet place to read and devote this time to yourself.

Who knows? You might just look back one day and realize this was the most important decision you ever made.

Welcome to the *Go 4 It!* club.

— Robert Pascuzzi
2018

CHAPTER 1

My *Go 4 It!* Story

Nobody can go back and start a new beginning, but anyone can start today and make a new ending.
Maria Robinson

Have you ever been at the jumping-off point, that painful place where you know for certain you just can't abide even one more day without making a dramatic, radical – unalterable – change in your life? Perhaps something that's been brewing in your gut for some time now?

I hope so, because, believe it or not, that pain is a gift – and it's just the medicine we all need to cause us to get our butts in gear and abandon our excuses. The fact is, we're all carrying around a nice big sack of BS. So, take a deep breath and inhale that lovely aroma one last time, because you are about to toss that sack and start to take hold of your life with both arms.

Let me reassure you that complete and total change is possible. I know that, because I was there myself just a few years ago.

This book is about you getting real with yourself, and, yes, we'll deal with some uncomfortable truths. The first truth is that it's about taking action in the moment – I mean today!

My first rude awakening came along just around the time I was turning 30, almost a quarter century ago.

Back then we grew up faster, and hitting 30 meant you were getting old. Bob Dylan famously said that we should "never trust anyone over 30," yet there I was, joining the ranks of the untrustworthy. I was thoroughly ensconced in my steady, though boring, job. Because I owned a house and a car, by the standards of my friends and family, things were just fine – but in fact, they really weren't.

Don't worry, I'm not going to unload another one of those "hitting bottom" tales on you, where I blather on about my war stories and misspent youth and how I crashed the car and the marriage, then finally, one day, had a spiritual awakening that allowed me to turn my life around. That's not my story, because, like most of us ... perhaps like you ... I was just happily trudging down the road of life, seeking comfort in mediocrity. After all, isn't that what we're all taught by our well-intentioned loved ones?

"If it ain't broke, don't fix it."

"Leave well enough alone."

"Be happy with what you have and stop complaining."

My friends and I mirrored and reinforced each other. Things were great if you had a few dollars in your pocket and a steady 9-to-5 job.

Don't get me wrong. I know that the vast majority of the world functions on some variation of this lifestyle, and it's fine for them; but I'm talking to you, and I suspect you picked up a book with a title like *Go 4 It!* because you are ready to challenge yourself.

As you read this book you might come up against some uncomfortable truths, and the first truth is that to change your life, you have to commit to taking action in your mind first. Yes, I said your mind first.

You can do anything you want with the one life you get, but at some point, you must promise yourself that you're not going back to the old you ... the old way of thinking and being ... and then find the leverage to ignite your will to make the necessary changes. If you have a burning desire – I'm talking about a real hunger– and the courage to embrace this way of thinking, you're *ready* to *Go 4 It!*

Will this be easy? Well, I'm here to tell you, it is easy to do if you're "all in." In other words, you must do the thing others may tell you are impossible. (Or perhaps it's really yourself doing the discouraging!) Once you do what others say you can't do, you'll never listen to their limitations again. Amazing things are not just possible, they are virtually guaranteed if you make the commitment, follow the directions, and develop the twin traits of courage and perseverance.

But it all *starts* with awareness.

Goals alone are not enough. If they were, we would simply have to "name it and claim it" and "see it and believe it." If it's that easy, why are people suffering? We all have been given the same mental faculties (the right stuff), but through negative programming from our upbringing, our environment, and social conditioning, we develop debilitating belief systems about what is possible in our lives. But these beliefs are not based in reality, they are based in the sum total of your decisions up to this point.

I'm not the guy who was voted "most likely to succeed" in my class! Not even close. A bagful of excuses and self-limiting beliefs weighed me down, and yet this unlikely character turned into a successful entrepreneur. I started from extremely humble beginnings and was your classic C student in high school and college, yet I'm now a partner in the number-one-rated wealth management firm in America.

This has been possible largely because I made a decision to commit to a life of personal development. I have devoted my adult life to studying countless methods of successful living, and through trial and error have discovered what works and what doesn't. You'll often hear entrepreneurs say that they would not trade in any of their hard-earned lessons, and you can count me among them. I value every challenge, every setback, every person who said I couldn't do it or wouldn't do it, because each of those experiences has shaped me and gifted me with some of my most valuable tools.

My goal with this book is to provide you with a blueprint for transformation that you can read in a weekend. How's that for a promise? Wake up on

Saturday morning as one person and completely turn your head around by Sunday night! You will get a plethora of practical information, loads of interesting stories, a few laughs, and links to some of the resources that have been most crucial to my *Go 4 It!* development. My plan is to give you all the tools you need to learn to truly live a *Go 4 It!* life and smash through the barriers, so that you will discover that these "barriers" are nothing more than paper tigers.

On the fast track to boredom

So, who am I and why should you listen to a guy who slipped through college and began his career as a lowly auto insurance claims adjuster?

My story is pretty typical. I went to a small college in Iowa. Right after graduation, I took the first job that was offered and found myself earning $17,500 a year. I was the fellow in a suit and tie would who comes along to inspect your car after an accident, and I was pretty good at it. It was a job, and I was comfortable, but I didn't realize that for me it was like being permanently anesthetized. This job was just good enough to be a really stealthy dream killer.

So, there I was, creeping through traffic on the

back roads of Des Moines, inspecting bumpers and reviewing police and medical reports and spending most of my time trying to figure out how to goof off and skip out early. If you had asked me what the favorite part of my job was, I would have said that I liked being out on the road because it gave me lots of freedom. By that I meant that I could set my own hours and had perfected the art of doing less while appearing to do more. If you're a traveling salesperson, you've probably perfected that dark art.

I genuinely liked meeting new people and I have always loved to negotiate, so that part was fun. It was a good day when I could work out a settlement that the home office thought was a win for the company. After a while, I got so good at it that the worst thing of all happened: They promoted me to supervisor!

Kansas City, here I come, and the next thing I know, I'm shackled to a gunmetal-gray desk in a cavernous room, with a bunch of other men and women in smart office attire all pushing paper while doing their absolute best to appear busy and engaged – though, based on the whining at the water cooler, it was obvious that none of us actually gave a darn about what we were doing.

The truth was, we would have done anything to end the boredom. Somehow, when you entered that room, it felt like you had stepped into a time warp, and by some mystical manipulation, the hands on the big clock on the wall would simply freeze in place. Then, finally, at precisely 4:55, the floor would suddenly erupt into a frenzy, with people chatting and smiling, as every poor soul in the place began shutting down their computers and getting ready to run out like the place was on fire.

Is it any wonder that the essence was oozing out of my soul, drop by precious drop? (And is it possible you might be able to identify with this experience?)

Several years went by and eventually I purchased a small house and a nice car and really didn't lack for much of anything, except for Kelly, the woman who was soon to enter my life. My friends and family all presumed I was well on my way in corporate America. I mean, in less than a decade, I was already on the second rung of the corporate ladder! Common sense dictated that I should not rock the boat. But something was stirring inside me, and no matter how hard I tried to quell that uncomfortable feeling, a question plagued me:

Is this all there is?

By my late 20s, I was voraciously reading and listening to inspirational self-help books, and I had even gone to a few motivational seminars. The problem was that, despite a bellyful of new knowledge, there was also a lifetime of old "tapes" constantly spinning in the back of my mind, and they were running the show. I had my own, built-in risk-management team that was constantly on duty, always at the ready to stamp out anything that would threaten the script on the tapes in my head that had, for decades, trained me to live and act a certain way.

Finally one day, things came to a head.

I was meeting with my boss for my annual salary review. Eric, the VP of auto claims for the Kansas City office, was a truly gentle soul with a big heart. I must have reminded him of one of his sons, because he just took a liking to me. As we were wrapping up the review, (and I learned I had earned a 3.5 percent annual increase), Eric grinned mischievously and told me he had some other good news. An office had opened up, and they were going to move me into it because I had been accepted into the "Future Leaders" program at the company. This meant the corporation had its eye on me, and, if things went as planned, I would be "fast-tracked." Eric leaned back in his chair and blew a perfect ring of smoke in the air. (Everyone smoked in the office back then.)

"You know what that means, don't you Bobby boy?"

"No, not really, but it sure sounds good," I said, pretending to be excited.

"Well, young man, after supervisor, you'll go on to regional manager, then manager, then director, then senior director, senior executive director, and, in 15 or 20 years, you might even be sitting in my chair – VP of the Claims Department!"

Of course, Eric was honestly trying to help me, because everything in his belief system told him that seeking security and stability should be *the* primary goal of life; but I remember thinking, as I shut the door to his office, that I had just been handed a death sentence.

I went out for drinks with a few buddies and they were apoplectic when I told them about the meeting and my doubts. "What the heck's the matter with you, Pascuzzi?!! You get a raise, move off the floor to an office, they tell you you're a rising star, and instead of being grateful, you get depressed! What sort of nut are you?"

These were all good, solid friends who had my best interests at heart. Maybe they were right. Maybe this is as good as it gets.

But something happened that night that changed the direction of my life.

No matter what I did, I couldn't fall asleep, and finally somewhere around 5 a.m., I went into the bathroom and stood peering into the mirror. At first I could hardly see my reflection, but with each passing moment, as the dawn began to rise, my image got clearer and clearer. It was as if I could see my future self, and I didn't like what I saw, because the guy looking back at me had simply allowed his essence to evaporate. Then suddenly I heard three simple words – and they rocked me.

"Go for it." Yes, that's right: YOU have a choice!

Now, that was scary… not just because I had heard a voice, but because the message was unquestionably the pure and simple truth. But, as we all know, just because we understand something intellectually, doesn't mean we will have the chops to do right thing, particularly when it's the hard thing. And

11

what exactly did "go for it" mean?

You cannot swim for new horizons until you have
the courage to lose sight of the shore.
William Faulkner

It didn't take me long to figure out that my future self was speaking to me for a reason, and it scared the crap out of me. I knew the meaning was that unless I quit my quit my job that very day, this moment would pass and I was likely to be sucked down a rabbit hole I could be stuck in for the rest of my life. That pain was the leverage I needed to actually do the thing I knew I needed to do!

Of course, such thoughts caused the "risk-management team" in my head to freak out and leap into action with their usual litany of stories they had at the ready, dishing out a healthy dose of fear and self-doubt.

"You're a complete idiot!

You were just given a raise and an office!" (The risk management team tends to exaggerate - it was really a big closet.)

"Why would you walk away from that?"

"I've heard a rumor you are in line for a company car, to boot!"

"You're going to turn down a vice presidency? Isn't that what you have been dreaming about since the day you joined the company?" (The same risk management team didn't mention I would be a lumpy old dude by the time that happened.)

"What are your friends going to say?"

"What about your parents? They are going to be so-o-o ashamed of you!" (The team in my head is good – they knew shame and guilt usually made me curl up into a fetal position.)

And then, the showstopper that could always excite my fear of complete and utter failure: "OK. Go ahead and quit this job. Then riddle me this: What are you going to do next? How are you going to pay the mortgage? Where will you live once you are on the street? I hope you like residing in an empty Maytag box!"

I'm sure you've figured out by now that despite all my negative self-talk, I handed in my notice that very day, and made my first go-for-it decision. I had to weather some pretty tough storms over the next several years, but I lived to fight another day. And

13

that's the point:

I woke up and came alive!

That's when I truly began my journey of self-discovery, which led to me to a life guided by a high degree of personal integrity and intention. The results have been extremely rewarding. I've not only benefited financially (and enjoy all the freedom that it brings), I am also blessed by a wonderful, loving family and relationships with many exceptional people.

As I write this, our world is in the midst of tremendous change. Some see the future as fearsome and bleak, but I think this is an extraordinary time to be alive. Technology today provides tools for business opportunities that our forefathers could scarcely have imagined. Just think what Henry Ford, John D. Rockefeller or Thomas Edison might have accomplished had they lived in the Internet age! But you and I are here, right now, and the promise of this magnificent future is ours for the taking.

So, this is it. The Big Show. Your moment to get off the sidelines and into the game. It's time to turn the page and learn how to *Go 4 It!*

CHAPTER 2
Go 4 It! or Go Home

*I'd rather regret the things I've done than
the things I haven't done.*
Lucille Ball

If you're expecting me to pick up the story from that
moment when I stormed out of my office in a blaze
of glory and went on to launch my *Go 4 It!* life and
strike it rich overnight, you came to the wrong place,
my friend.

Sure, I could tell you that, but then this book
would just be one of those Hollywood-ending, inspirational self-help books meant to stroke your delicate
ego so you won't experience a bad feeling and just
turn tail and run.

So, let me be clear with you. If you're afraid of
some naked honesty, and expect a participation tro-

phy just for showing up and turning the page, then you might as well toss this book into the nearest dumpster. My goal is nothing less than to show you how to achieve amazing things in your life – presuming you hold up your end of the bargain, which is to put the work in ... today and over the long haul. Keep in mind, however that I said I would *provide the tools*. If tools sit on the shelf gathering dust, they are worthless. However, put them to use (and learn how to use them properly) and you will finally make the changes you have been putting off. That's what the *Go 4 It!* plan is all about.

Let's start with some raw honesty: We humans rarely make a change unless we are experiencing pain.

The human brain has many ways of convincing us that things are just fine even when life is actually pretty miserable. Psychologists and psychiatrists have lots of expensive names for this, such as "resistance," "purposeful forgetting," "avoidance behavior," and "denial." These are the kinds of thoughts that allow us to suck down a bowl of ice cream even though our gut is pouring over our pants. Instant gratification will usually win out, but the cumulative effect can be deadly. I'm not saying I'm any different. After

I quit my job as a claims adjuster, I lulled myself into complacency for a few years, until I was in a world of hurt, but I chose not to see it.

I had switched industries, gotten married, had three kids, and was just barely able to afford the mortgage and car payments. Every month was a struggle because I was in sales and my compensation was based 100 percent on commissions. Some months I did really well, and other months I had to write a check to the company.

We were barely getting by, but I had convinced myself that we were comfortable. *Comfortable*, I now know, is a bad place to be, and simply another way of saying complacent. And that's just another word for *inertia*, which is the fastest track to nowhere.

My moment of pain, or my personal bottom, came when I hit a few bad months in a row and suddenly we weren't able to pay the bills. But what really hurt the most was when I had to ask Kelly, my wife, to go down to the bank and put our mortgage payment on a credit card.

I remember the tears in her eyes that day, and that did it. For me, there is no greater humiliation than not being able to take care of my family.

This experience pushed me beyond the usual mental suffering I had been willing to endure, into a state of agony; it forced me over the edge, and that's when it became evident that I had had enough. I decided to change my entire attitude about money.

Getting to a place where you say to yourself, "I have had it!" is an amazing turning point in your life.

I determined that I would no longer act like a paralyzed, fearful wimp about my finances but would instead embrace an attitude of abundance (which I'll explain in detail later in the book). That mental shift enabled me to focus on the solution rather than allowing doubt to control me.

As soon as I made that committed, mental shift, I began to see opportunities where I had previously only seen problems. And, amazingly, from that day forth, little by little, things began to improve.

It definitely did not happen overnight.

However, because of my go-for-it attitude, I was unwilling to give up. I began crafting a new path for myself, one that I enjoyed. Many friends and relatives tried to convince me otherwise, out of concern for me, but I didn't succumb to the "comfortable" way, because that way just wasn't for me. I had developed the ability to live with uncertainty and perseverance, and so I just kept on moving forward. Of course, it wasn't easy to do, but it is what all successful people must learn to do.

I can guarantee that life will throw obstacles your way. Learn to deal with them, and you will succeed. Put your head in the sand and all hell will break loose sooner or later.

To cut to the chase, I eventually switched fields and moved into the business of selling 401K plans, and that's where I found my sweet spot. But first, I still had to endure some growing pains.

About 14 years ago, I was fortunate enough to join Creative Planning Inc. Fast-forward to 2018, and we are now the number one wealth management company in America! Today, my phone rings off the hook, and my email pings with inquiries all day long, but back then (and for many years following), my life was one endless stream of cold calls, and the usual response was "Bob who?"

Yes, some days were miserable back then, and there were many moments when I thought of tossing in the towel. But I was no longer lingering in the negative.

We never know when things are going to turn around, but take it from me – they do. Have patience, make one good decision after the next, and develop faith in the future, yourself, and your higher power.

I've taken the time to give you this capsule history of my business career, to let you know it didn't come easy.

If you're reading this and thinking, "This dude's got a nice success story, but how's that going to help me make payroll next week?" Trust me, I've been there.

Or if you're thinking, "This lucky guy is flying around in a corporate jet, but I'm mopping the floor at McDonald's; he doesn't know jack about my life" … well, you should know that one of my first jobs was literally in a sewer. My boss would send me down into a hole in the ground, so I could crawl around – knee deep in you-know-what – and clean out the pipes – all for the princely sum of $4.50 an hour! Sure, it was a long time ago, and I was a college kid, but the experience helped shape me. Each shovelful taught me about accountability. I had to pay my tuition, and that was the best job I could get at the time. I also learned that, no matter what the weather, or whether I had the sniffles, when the bell rang, I had to suit up and show up. Those nasty sewers weren't going to unclog themselves!

There's no doubt that my parents instilled a great work ethic in me, and for that I will be forever grateful; but it wasn't until I looked in the mirror that morning and gave myself a good kick in the butt that I finally got honest enough to start to make fundamental changes.

The key?
I stopped constantly mulling things over
and took action.

I knew it wasn't going to be easy, but, as you'll recall, I actually quit my job that day, despite the fact that I didn't have another source of income or much of a nest egg. I did that because I knew, with absolute certainty, that to do otherwise would be a disservice to the most precious thing I possess: my life.

The purpose of life is to do all you can
with all you've been given.
Jim Rohn

I was almost 30 when I made my go-for-it decision. You may be older or younger. It doesn't matter. Why? Because the only day we have is today, and our age is irrelevant. A famous Jim Rohn quote puts it more succinctly: "If you really want to do something, you'll find a way. If you don't, you'll find an excuse."

Let's break out the shovels

Before we can get to our truth, we have to clear the garbage out of our brains. This begins by exposing the primary BS stories we've been telling ourselves.

Actually, we get so accustomed to first hearing these stories about ourselves (parents, peers, coaches and teachers all have their loud opinions in our formative years), that we don't even notice that we're telling ourselves these stories. At some point, it becomes this unconscious kind of litany … it's when the "risk management team" steps in and just sets up a sort of trip alarm for itself. This "team" or "tapes" are, in more scientific terms, **paradigms** that operate at a very unconscious level in your life … until you trip over their carefully-wired alarm system, that is.

In my case, despite years of self-study, including numerous live seminars, my own paradigms had me unconsciously clinging to my precious self-limiting narratives that allowed procrastination to rule my thinking. Procrastination is deadly because it operates in the dark recesses of your mind. I couldn't see it at the time, but whenever I would make a serious attempt at living my authentic life, my personal BS stories (paradigms) would mysteriously surface.. The trip alarm was blaring, and the risk management team was, once again, leaping into action with its two no-fail arguments:

1. I'm not smart enough.
2. What if I don't have enough money?

Of course, these were not my only self-limiting beliefs; I had many more, but these two items were the dominant ones, at the top of my list. Each came from the same basic place: fear. My brain's risk management team was in full, frenzied gallop in my head, its only intent to keep me stuck right in my comfort zone.

You have your own set of self-limiting beliefs, and it's now almost time to write them down and shine the light of truth on them, but first, let's take a moment to consider this quote from Jim Morrison, someone who embodied the *Go 4 It!* philosophy:

**"Expose yourself to your deepest fear.
After that, you are free."**

Now, there is some truth. How do we know? If you genuinely embrace this concept, it will make you feel uncomfortable – and, contrary to popular belief, it's a good thing to feel uncomfortable. When you feel that discomfort you know you're winning over the pre-taped, long standing paradigms in your own head.

**A person who decides to go for it will
enthusiastically jump into the unknown.
Risk.
Take a chance.
Possibly fail.**

If you really go for it, then you know that you will, without a doubt, fail sometimes. In fact, you'll undoubtedly fail more often than you succeed at the beginning. Don't be a crybaby; just learn from the lessons put before you, and move on!

Let's get with the program now and list the changes you know you need to make. Think about work, relationships, health, or whatever else you know you need to deal with in a very different way, but have been resisting.

Don't just select something that's easy to do. I'm talking about changing something – doing something that you know is going to be life transforming. Think about it, but don't let any doubts creep in and spook you. Now, write down your top three. You know what they are. Get up and *Go 4 It!*

1. _____FINANCES_____

2. _____WORK_____

3. ___RELATIONSHIPS (Romantic)___

Now, here's the mind-blowing part: We're going to anticipate your self-limiting beliefs and head them off at the pass. For each item you would like to accomplish, tap into the risk management team in YOUR head and write down what they've started whispering to you ... I'm betting it begins with something like the following ...

"I'm not: WELL KNOWN ENOUGH TO GET THE ACTING WORK I DESIRE."

"What if: I HAVE TO DECLARE BANKRUPTCY AND REBUILD MY LIFE AT 40"

"I'll wait because: I'M JUST PARALYZED WHERE I STAND BECAUSE I DON'T KNOW WHAT TO DO"

Make a definite decision

Now that you have listed three things you would like to change, I'd like you to choose the one that you know is going to be life-altering. To quote Jim Morrison again, this is the decision that will allow you to "break on through to the other side."

What one item in your list really scares you – you

have absolutely no idea how you can ever reach or obtain it?

That's the one.

It's the one that, once achieved, is going to make a radical improvement for the rest of your life. I call this your *Definite Decision*. Please write it on the lines below, sign it, and add today's date:

I WILL NEVER BE PARALYZED, GRIPPED WITH FEAR, AND DOUBT, WITH LIMITING BELIEFS, MY FINANCIAL LIFE AGAIN. I WILL CHOOSE ABUNDANCE OVER LACK, POSSIBILITY OVER LIMITATION AND ACHIEVE FINANCIAL FREEDOM FOR THE BETTERMENT OF ME AND MY FAMILY, AND THE WORLD.

Signature _____

Date _MONDAY, DECEMBER 23, 2019_

27

Take a moment to check in on how you feel right now, having made your Definite Decision. Feels pretty powerful, right?

Now that you've made the decision, it's only a matter of time before you turn it into a reality. As we proceed in this book, I'm going to break this down and show you how to succeed. This is a big gulp, so you have to take it in pieces, and you will need to develop some skills. Hang in there, and read on, because we are going to do this together.

Planning vs. envisioning

I have put a great deal of time into distilling this message into a plan that you can read in a few short hours. I've cut out the extraneous material because I want to convince you to seize this day and make it the day you look back on and know you took the right turn in the road.

It's my belief that we have to put all our focus and energy into what we're doing at the moment. Long-term planning sounds good, but long-term envisioning of your end result ... where you want to be living and experiencing your life after achieving your success ... is even better. Why? Because as you start out on this new path, things might not seem to go according to your plan. Going for broke means that we charge after what's in front of us at the moment, trusting that the better end result we picture daily WILL happen. The future tends to take care of itself when we are excited, moving and doing what we know to do to act on the new vision in our heads.

Vision without action is merely a dream.
Action without vision just passes time.
Vision with action can change the world.
Joel A. Barker

Remember, there's just no way to anticipate all the hurdles you will encounter, so don't waste your time imagining all the things that could go wrong.

A *Go 4 It!* life requires courage to persist when the going gets tough. Nothing that is difficult to achieve happens overnight, so it's important to develop a hunger and passion that will sustain you through the inevitable challenges and setbacks.

Now that you know what you want to change, get excited about it and move it up to the front burner. Here's the next exercise to really solidify your Definite Decision. Please don't skip over it or tell yourself you'll come back later (that's the risk management team up to its usual whispering).

Back to your future

This exercise is simple yet incredibly valuable. Please take a few moments to read the next few paragraphs slowly and thoughtfully.

Imagine you are at specific point in the future, say, 10 years from now, and you have long since abandoned the Definite Decision you made today. Perhaps you started to lose weight, but then gave up after a few months, and gained it all back, plus much more, and now avert your eyes from the mirror when you climb out of the shower. Or maybe you decided to quit your dead-end job and launch the company of your dreams, but chickened out at the thought of losing your regular paycheck. Now, each morning when you plop into your same old chair, you lose another ounce of self-respect. Or perhaps the nasty habit you committed to discard has mushroomed into a full-blown addiction, and now you feel desperate and hopeless.

Whatever your Definite Decision was today has been swallowed in the haze of time; though you can't remember exactly when you undid your Definite Decision, because it happened, drip by drip. A decade from now, you notice this book on the shelf, open it, and run your finger across the words you wrote today; and your regret reaches right down to the very core of your being.

Or, on the other hand ...

Imagine that you are at a specific point in the future, say, 10 years from now, and you have long since achieved the Definite Decision you made today. You lost the weight, continued to eat correctly and exercise daily, and you feel younger than you did a decade ago. Now you pause when you climb out the shower and love to see your reflection in the mirror. Or perhaps you created that company you just knew was inside of you and today you have freedom, financial security, and the pride of having done something difficult and important. You cherish every obstacle you overcame because each one makes the satisfaction of your achievement that much richer. Or you think of the nasty habit you abandoned 10 years ago and realize you haven't had the desire to do that self-destructive thing for years. You blew through your ini-

tial goal and then built on that success. And you can trace the beginning of this transformation to this very day and the energy that was generated the moment you committed to your Definite Decision.

How do you feel? How do the people you love feel about you? How has the world been enhanced because of you?

Reread the second scenario one more time, and try to identify with the feelings, even though the particular ideas may differ. Then close your eyes and think of your Definite Decision. Take a few moments to bathe in the reality of your achievement, your end result. See with utter clarity that it is just a matter of how firmly you commit, how quickly you recognize self-limiting mantras that are trying to hold you back, and how wisely you use your time. Sit still for a few minutes. Believe it has happened, and it has changed everything about you – how you move and talk, how you relate to everyone in your life. Your entire being has been transformed. Just sit still and place yourself at that moment in the future,

And now ... make the commitment to go for broke.

The *Go 4 It!* Commitment

I, _____KYLE LOWDER_____, on this
name
the 23ʳᵈ day of _____DECEMBER_____, 2019, here-
month
by commit to my Definite Decision. I do this despite
the certainty I will encounter real challenges and obstacles and even imagined obstacles from "risk management team" in my head. When difficulties arise, I
will be grateful for them because I know that I can
only learn and grow by overcoming adversity and
that all setbacks are temporary. Furthermore, I acknowledge that I am fortunate to live in a time where
I have been granted the freedom to make mistakes
and recover accordingly and should, therefore, live
my life in a spirit of gratitude, generosity, patience,
and good humor. I will remain focused and resolute
with the indomitable will that my Creator has given
me, certain in the knowledge that I have been blessed
with a life of great abundance.

Signature_____

33

CHAPTER 3
Incoming! *(Storm Shelter Might be Required)*

Now that you've made your Definite Decision, I have to warn you about something. You might be that truly rare person who sails right past this, but my experience says that most of the people reading this book are going to run into this pretty quickly ...

You know that risk management team in your head – that set of paradigms that has been running along unconsciously, formatting your life, keeping you safely and securely away from that Definite Decision you just made?

As noted previously, once you start even *considering* a Definite Decision, those tripwires are going to start blaring. "Stop! Go no further! Take one step more and you're risking life and limb!"

Once you DO make the Definite Decision, however, and truly commit to it, ... the sensible voices and urgent whispers in your head are going to turn up the volume to an ear-splitting 3-alarm fire siren. Suddenly, the risk management team is calling for all-hands on deck to rise up and quell your Definite Decision.

In short, my friend, expect a military strike from your paradigms.

These guys have been in charge of your life longer than you can remember. They might have dropped into your infant or early childhood mind before you even had the ability to recognize the thought, let alone combat it. Soon a habitual way of thinking was formed and, in some cases, it truly did keep you out of harm's way (i.e., look both ways before crossing the street, never put your hand on a hot stove, don't stick your finger in that socket, stop teasing your big brother).

Then, other paradigms piled on during your schooling, your early work experiences, relationships and more. Begun as just a comment or even a look sometimes, these thoughts about yourself and what you could achieve worked their way into your habitual way of thinking.

Paradigms can be invigorating and supportive – in fact, that's exactly what you're doing here with help from these unfolding *Go 4 It!* chapters – you're in-stilling healthier, life-invigorating paradigms in your mind.

But, in many cases, you've developed habitu-al ways of thinking that have proven to NOT serve your bigger life, your bigger dreams. As I noted in the previous chapter ... you can probably think back to times in your life when you made a commitment and, then, a few months later, discovered you hadn't really followed through with the plan. For some reason, it just got to be too hard. After a litany of excuses, you lapsed back into the same old you (which is hardly a bad thing, but when you're wanting growth and expansion for your life, the same old you can be a mighty disappointing person to see in your bathroom mirror).

The litany of excuses are your paradigms. When you make your Definite Decision, they're going to start rolling in from all sides like a well-planned mil-itary strike.

The key is to stay on track. Nothing these para-digms can lob at you can take you down ... unless you let them. When you make a Definite Decision, you mean business. You're not going back. You're not changing your mind.

Don't listen to the buzzards

In my observation, successful people have an in-nate or developed skill that allows them to reach deci-sions quickly and change decisions slowly. They also surround themselves with people who are knowledge-able in their field and avoid others with unsubstanti-ated opinions. This is who YOU are and who you're becoming. Never doubt this.

So, here's my second warning: When you decide to live a *Go 4 It!* life, expect that others will question your judgment. When they do, consider the source. Sometimes people are well-intentioned, sometimes they aren't. Some suggestions have value, most do not.

If the suggestion is coming from someone who loves you, it may be well-intentioned, but they may be speaking their fear to you. Remember, they have their own set of paradigms, too, and they might just happen to like the arrangement you have with one another just the way it is.

I like to say that it's important not to hang with or listen to "the buzzards." Look around and you will find them everywhere. They might be good friends, family relations or associates, or they could be some random stranger popping up on your Facebook page.

If you know in your gut that you have made the right decision, don't be easily dissuaded. As my mentor, Bob Proctor says, "Don't allow someone else to steal your dream."

You've got to keep your oars in the water and keep rowing. Prepare yourself in advance so that when you're set upon by the paradigm military strike or the buzzards, you're staying on track.

For me, I came up with a number of short affirmations that I could reel off anytime the sirens in my head went off:

"I am living the life I've envisioned."

"I am courageous."

"I am abundant."

"I am relaxed and at peace."

"Everything good comes my way."

I am focused, energetic, magnetic, honest ..." You get the picture.

Another preemptive strike involves that visualization of your end result. Write it out repeatedly, having already achieved it. Pull photos from magazines.

Step into the lifestyle in some way or form. Do whatever it takes to craft that stellar, clear-as-day image so that you can *immediately* start reeling it in your head when the old paradigms start the howling siren nonsense.

As you move forward on your Definite Decision, you might discover that the evidence (in the form of results) demonstrates that you need to make a course correction. This is perfectly fine. As Napoleon Hill noted decades ago, a ship's captain will make many small adjustments in the ship's course based on compass readings that have assured him of arrival in a specified port. You're entitled to course corrections, especially if they promise a smoother, possibly faster course of knowledge and experience that you can rely upon to reach your end goal.

Rally your supporters

We live in an amazing time where there is an enormous amount of excellent information at our fingertips (much of it free) and many fabulous teachers, and you should avail yourself of that information.

As an example, I love Lou Holtz. With a 249–132–7 record, Coach Holtz is one of the most successful college football coaches in history. He is always striving to improve himself and everyone around him, and has said that one of the keys to success is to surround yourself with people who are ahead of you in terms of where you want to be. You should always be going where the expectations are high. It's almost impossible for your ego to be in control when you are constantly surrounded by high achievers, who will suggest a slight alteration in your course with only the best of intentions in mind for you, and encourage you to push yourself forward.

*Successful people will always tell you that
you can do something. It's the people who have
never accomplished anything who will
always discourage you.*
Lou Holtz

CHAPTER 4
Live with Intention

Every thought we think is creating our future.
Louise Hay

I'm going to give you the benefit of the doubt and presume you did some significant work in the first chapter in setting your Definite Decision and creating a moat of positive affirmation around it. Great, you are off to an excellent start!

On the other hand, if you just thumbed through the pages and decided to put off making a decision till "some other day," then I can guarantee that you will fail. That piece of information should force you to rise up and say something like, "No. Not this time. This time I will actually achieve success."

So, if you need to, go back NOW and return here when you're done, we'll wait …

I recently gave a talk to a group of high school seniors as they were preparing to head off to college. Much of what I had to say dealt with how they were going to be confronted with difficult choices on a daily basis. Of course, they were used to hearing this type of admonition from adults – how this is a precarious time in the life of every young person, and so on. I did my best to encourage this group to recognize how fortunate they each were to have this opportunity to seize the moment in a positive way, and told them some stories about my past to try to keep it interesting.

They were a smart group of kids, who asked some excellent questions, most of which I fielded without too much trouble. Then one young man stood up and asked a question that stumped me.

"Mr. Pascuzzi, if you were a product, what would your brand be?"

Off the top of my head I replied something about working hard, sticking to it during tough times, being mentally and physically fit, keeping a positive attitude, hanging with the right crowd, and even mentioned having a go-for-it mentality. Inwardly, I had to admit that I didn't really know my "brand."

Live with Intention

It was actually a great question, and I knew what he was looking for – a brief description – my raison d'être in just a few words. I guess he thought that a guy my age, who had achieved some success, would have some high degree of self-awareness and would have the answer at the ready. If you asked me that question about Creative Planning, it would be easy for me to answer, because we are all about putting our customers' interests above our own.

It plagued me that I didn't really have a clear and simple understanding about my essential nature. I started asking friends and relatives what they thought my "brand" was, and, after looking at me sideways (because they had never asked themselves this question), they all came back with the same set of general characteristics that had occurred to me. It wasn't until a few days later that my wife, Kelly, got it exactly right.

"You know, Bob, you're all about living your life with intention.

"I don't think I've ever met anyone as disciplined and focused as you are, and I've watched you work at it over the years, and seen how far you've come; I know how determined you are," she said.

"Sometimes it drives me nuts, but I know you are on a mission, and I think that's the word that defines you: *intention*. You live with intention."

I leapt out of my chair, looked to the sky, and shouted: "Yes! That's it! You said it! And the key to living with intention is to control our minds!" Kelly is used to me by now, so she wasn't surprised when I ran over to hug her and then danced around the room in glee. I knew I had just been smacked upside the head with a dose of good old-fashioned *Truth*.

My mind was popping with a thousand thoughts, and I knew I had to sit down and write about it. I sat back, closed my eyes, and focused. The thought I had just shouted out a moment before came to mind:

The key to living with intention is to
control our thinking.

I took a few deep breaths, and thought about the real meaning of that statement. Suddenly, things clicked into place and I realized the answer was obvious. *Just describe how you live, what you actually do every single day. Don't worry whether or not people will judge you!*

My Typical *Go 4 It!* Day

Here it is – the process for daily living that I have developed through years of trial and error. Each day actually starts the night before.

BEDTIME

In the evening, before going to bed, I select the clothes I will be wearing for work the next day. In that way I'm up and dressed, teeth brushed, and out the door in 20 minutes. Compare that approach to what most people do – leaving the clothing selection until morning and fumbling around in the dark, make a rushed decision, and beginning the day in a stressful state. (Not to mention that there is a lot to be said about dressing with intention, but that's a whole other topic.) This simple process of preparation puts my mind at ease; it positions me for the next day with a sense of confidence and preparedness. My armor is out and I am ready to do battle.

Right before going to sleep, I'll read something of a positive or spiritual nature for 10 to 20 minutes and then turn out the light and go through my I AM list as I doze off. These are the last thoughts I want cascading through my mind at night as I head off to dreamland.

"I AM all-knowing."

"I AM all-powerful."

"I AM courageous."

"I AM abundant."

"I AM a giver."

"I AM young."

"I AM focused, energetic, magnetic, honest, persuasive, a lover . . ."

Now, you may find this technique a little weird, but I think it's criminal that most people allow negative thoughts to flood their minds when they climb into bed.

Think about it. Is that the best time to worry about paying the bills or what's going on with the kids? Do you pick that moment to fret over something you didn't do that day or need to do the next day? If you need to do something the next day, write it down on your to-do list and accept that you will take care of it the next day. Your purpose in going to bed is to sleep and to rejuvenate your body, so keep heading in that direction. Don't allow the final thoughts you have before you fall asleep to be fear-based or worrisome, because that will impact your subconscious mind.

Is it any wonder that so many people struggle with sleep? Take control of your mind and soothe your brain with whatever positive affirmations fit you best. Think about all you have to be grateful for, and focus on those things as well as all of your attributes. If a negative thought starts to creep in, smack it down and return to your positive affirmations. Drift off to sleep with a sense of peace, confidence and enthusiasm for the next day, because you are powerful and you are prepared!

The best thing about the future is that it comes only one day at a time.
Abraham Lincoln

MORNING

On a normal workday, my alarm is set for 5:10. When the alarm goes off, I'm welcomed into the day with what I call a *Go 4 It!* moment. This is the first of many choices we will be confronted with that day. Are we going to hit the snooze button or are we going to bounce up? I'm only human and I know that the flesh is weak, particularly early in the morning, when we're nice and comfy under our warm blankets, so

I have devised what I call the 7-Second Rule. This works for me, and I know it will work for you, so just give it a try. Count to 7, then say, "It's time to GO," throw off the covers, and get out of bed.

In this way, you are beginning the day by making an immediate positive statement to yourself. You will be in control of your mind, not the other way around. Don't give your mind the option of staying in bed beyond the count of seven! It's sort of the same philosophy as doing a cannonball into a pool. Just GO for it. You're about to get wet anyway, why just stick a toe in the water?

Obviously some days are harder than others, depending on how much sleep you've gotten and a host of other factors, but let's face facts – you are going to have to get out of bed eventually. Are those extra 15 minutes really going to make a difference? Maybe not – except that the delay may cause you to run late, or have to rush, and that means you will be starting the day off under stress.

Do yourself a favor and adopt the 7-Second Rule. Starting the day with intention will set the table for a positive day.

By the way, the most important word in the *Go*

4 It! attitude is GO! Those two little letters hold tremendous power. Keep them at the forefront of your mind throughout the day. This tiny, little word is an incredible tool if used properly. Remember that your mind is always going to throw up objections, but you can crash through those walls. When the time comes to get out of bed, set that new goal, head to the gym, sit down to have that talk with a spouse or teenager, or enter a difficult negotiation ...

Go 4 It! people focus on GO.

It's the GO that jump-starts us and puts us in motion.

Next, after I throw on my gym clothes, I put on my headphones and brush my teeth with the music pumping through my body. My playlist gives me power that feeds my mind and tells my body to GO, especially when I don't feel like it.

Now, let's look at what just happened. Just five minutes ago, I was sound asleep, and now I have totally changed my state from a place of complete inertia to being fully engaged in the day. The only reason I was able to literally seize the day is due to intentional living. I know what I'm going to wear the next day. I have an iPhone next to my bed, filled with music that I am certain is going to rock my soul, and I have a system that I follow that will start me up.

You'll notice that the process I've created has eliminated any possibility that my mind can sneak in and take over while I am in a weakened (sleeping) condition.

Let's remember the lessons learned in the first chapter. If we allow our minds to sucker us in with our own unique "risk management" stories, they will. Remember that negative tapes are running in the background 24/7, and unless you have a plan to circumvent them, they will creep in like thieves in the night. For instance, here are a few "good" reasons they will give you for pressing the snooze button:

"It's cold (or hot) outside. I feel really good right here."

"I'll just sleep in for another 15 minutes, then head to the gym."

And then, after 15 minutes: "I'll just head to the gym after work, or at lunchtime."

Do any of these excuses sound familiar? Of course they do, that's how all of our minds work.

The problem is that, before you know it, instead of putting together seven days of working out, you've put together seven days of sleeping in. Bad habits are easier to reinforce (and harder to break) than good ones.

I make a point of arriving at the gym by 6 a.m. or earlier. It should be obvious to you by now that I believe that the relationship between a positive mind and a healthy body is a primary factor in success – it may even be *the* primary factor in achieving success, and I will be devoting an entire chapter to that later in the book. For now I just want to touch on my daily process.

When I arrive at the gym, I start the day by building muscle, discipline, and stamina. The music is pounding in my ears, again helping to power my mind and body to GO, especially when I don't feel like it. By pushing through and repeating the process, even the most challenging situations can become par for the course.

For me, starting my day at the gym is the foundation for the rest of my day. I've had days where I was at the gym at 3:30 a.m. to get my workout in because I had to catch an early-morning flight. But it wasn't always easy for me, and I realize that change is difficult, but the very fact that you are reading this book, and have already made a Definite Decision indicates that you are on your way. We all have to start at some point, and this is your new beginning, so hop on the *Go 4 It!* Express, I guarantee it will be an exciting ride!

Go 4 It! people are 100 percent committed – there's no in between.

Columbus didn't say, "We're turning back if we don't see land in another two days."

NASA didn't say, "Aw, shucks, I guess we'll stop trying for the moon.

THE WORKDAY – Thought Conditions

For breakfast, I like to keep it simple with a protein shake or a few hardboiled eggs, and I usually arrive at the office by around 7:45 a.m.

During the day at work I use some "thought conditioners," which I have taped to my desk and look at occasionally. These are just quick, easy reminders and affirmations to help keep me on track, especially when some unexpected storm pops up. Here's one of mine.

Live with Intention

*If anyone advances confidently in the direction
of his dreams, and endeavors to live the life
which he has imagined, he will meet with a
success unexpected in common hours.*
Henry David Thoreau

Choose a few that connect with you and place them where they can easily be seen throughout the day. Life will always be filled with surprises. Don't let the surprises deter you – just stay on track with that Definite Decision in the forefront of my mind.

When you have to deal with the unexpected, it's important not to allow emotion to rule your response. We all get upset. Just get back on track and focus on the solution.

When confronted with a problem, I like to use my 7-Second Rule so that I won't dwell on the negative too long.

For instance, let's say something happens – perhaps a deal falls through. Sure, I'm not happy; that's just a natural reaction. If I didn't have that reaction, I would just be denying my genuine emotions. But I don't have to allow it to taint, or perhaps ruin, the day. So, if I have determined that we have exhausted all options and the deal cannot be revived, the key is to use the 7-Second Rule and allow myself that little amount of time to be irritated, annoyed, frustrated, or whatever. Then pop out of it and say, "Okay, let's GO! On to the next opportunity!"

And guess what? There are always other opportunities.

If you allow yourself to carry around resentments or feel irritated all day, then it will negatively impact the quality of the decisions you make throughout the day. When I notice that I am bothered by something, but I can't quite put my finger on it, I'll stop and search my mind. When I discover what's troubling me, I'll ask myself again if I have done all I can to solve the problem. If I haven't, I will take an action. If I have, then I let it go.

After work, if I'm not away on a business trip, I like to take the dog for a walk with my wife, Kelly. There's a nice lake close to our home with a beautiful walking trail, and I find nothing as refreshing as being surrounded by nature and being with the people I love. Yes, I actually do like to relax; it's essential for life balance. And I love to sleep. I do have a rule, however, that before I go to bed I always return every email that has been sent to me throughout the day. Occasionally I'm up later than planned, but normally I'm under the covers with an inspirational book by 11 p.m.

Develop your *Go 4 It!* day

We each have to devise our own plans, and I know that I may seem to be on the extreme side. But it's my goal to push you to do another rep, or run another lap, or instigate the 7-Second Rule during your day, regardless of how you spend your day or what kind of work you do. The 7-Second Rule works just as beautifully for moms who are negotiating all day with their toddlers as it does for people in skyscrapers negotiating their work deals.

Each individual needs to decide where they are on their path, and make the decision to *Go 4 It!* in a way that will be successful for them personally. Knowing you can do it will get you to your goal. Perhaps you've led a sedentary life and you aren't about to jump out of bed and run to the gym, but I'll bet that you could use the 7-Second Rule when the alarm goes off tomorrow. I can tell you that if you make just that one commitment, right now, it will improve your life.

THE 7 SECOND RULE

When my alarm goes off tomorrow morning, I will count to 7, and get out of bed to start the day.

Signature _____ 12/23/19

Now let's give you another gift; an extra 20 minutes of life tomorrow.

Just think: By adding a mere 20 minutes to your life in the morning and filling that time with something that balances, centers or moves you forward on your Definite Decision path in some way, you will be adding at least 10 hours of newly productive time each month!

THE 20 MINUTE RULE

I will rise 20 minutes earlier than my usual time tomorrow and I will use that time in a positive, productive manner. I could do some inspirational reading, or get some exercise, or perhaps listen to my Creator or nature, or maybe I will prepare some healthy food, so I can avoid eating junk food later in the day.

Signature _____ 12/23/19

Long-term Intentions

I've just walked you through a typical workday for me, and given you a few key ideas that you should be able to easily incorporate into your life. Hopefully you signed and dated the 7-Second and 20-Minute rules, I've asked you to make those two tiny commitments in order to demonstrate just how easy it is to take control of that one commodity that is always slipping away: time.

It's obvious that making this change for one day is not actually going to have any impact on your life. However, if you make even just these minor changes at the very beginning of the day, on a regular basis, and you develop the discipline to stick with it EVERY day, it will dramatically improve how you approach and use each day.

I've seen this work for me and I know it's because I'm starting the day by taking control of my mind before it has a chance to take control of me. Our minds are pernicious buggers, and left to their own devices they will always scream, "Just roll over and snooze for another 10 minutes," or "What are you worrying about? Eat the cookie! Here, have another! You deserve it!"

However, it's important to be realistic and admit that we will occasionally get off track. That's okay. It only means that we have to look at each day as an entirely new opportunity. Don't give up.

CHAPTER 5

Change Your Perspective

Time is free, but it's priceless.
You can't own it, but you can use it.
You can't keep it, but you can spend it.
Once you've lost it, you can never get it back.
Your time is limited, so don't waste it living
someone else's life.
Steve Jobs

We are the only species on earth that has the intellectual ability to contemplate our own mortality. And while we may not like to dwell on the subject, somewhere in our psyche we are aware our Creator has allotted us just so many breaths. That means, on the most basic level, the only thing we possess is time, yet we don't know how much of it we have been allotted. So, how we use our time is fairly significant, wouldn't you say? In order to live your life with intention, you must learn to change what you do with your time.

Notice, I didn't write that you have to CONTROL your time. The great motivational speaker Earl Nightingale once noted that "time can't be controlled and it can't be managed" ... only tasks can be controlled and managed in the timeframe you've been allotted each day.

In my previous *"Live With Intention"* chapter 1 introduced you to the concept of changing what you do with your time with the tasks that you choose. These intentional tasks range from organizing your day the evening prior to putting the 7-Second Rule into practice and building in physical exercise and balance to your day.

Once you have made a firm and Definite Decision, you're going to find that your approach to goal-oriented tasks is going to change, too. When you are driven with a *Go 4 It!* Attitude, you will likely discover that you've been doing all sorts of daily tasks that have nothing to do with your Definite Decision.

Granted, we all have mundane tasks we must attend to in a day, but the action steps that are necessary for your movement forward MUST be the priority. Even more important than laying out your clothes the evening prior is taking a few minutes to organize the next day's tasks so that you are always focused on moving closer to your end goal.

Now, here's the rub: You may be absolutely excelling at prioritizing and acting on that change you want in your life ... you're doing and acting on a daily basis, making these tasks the first priority in your day ... and nothing seems to be happening.

We've all heard the saying "Time takes time." This is a phrase I keep in mind when I am feeling impatient about a situation. While I might have an idea on how quickly this all needs to come together for me, there is an unseen, germinating energy to my every goal – and it might not be operating on my timeline. The vital key to keep in mind is simply this:

Don't quit. Don't give up.
You've planted the seed in the soil and
you're watering it daily.
There is no doubt that it will
eventually sprout.

I'm not the most patient person in the world, so I need to do some positive things that keep me focused on the eventual outcome … that place where I will ultimately arrive. Another tool that I've developed is what I call my *"Change Your Perspective"* process. It's based upon a personal experience.

You'll recall that earlier I mentioned I hit a point in my life that caused me to radically change my attitude about money. That was the day several years ago when there was just too much month at the end of the money, and my wife had to put our mortgage payment on a credit card. It became apparent to me right then that I had to change my relationship to money or, more specifically, my fears about never having enough. That's easy to say, but how does one actually do it?

Well, in my case, on the night in question, after Kelly and I had discussed the situation ad nauseam, I escaped downstairs to the isolation of my home office so I could lick my wounds and feel sorry for myself. (Self-pity is about the most unproductive use of time, by the way!)

This was the place in my home where I paid the bills (or rather, avoided paying the bills.) Actually, the bald truth is that I had taken to stuffing them in a folder and hiding them in the back of my filing cabinet where they couldn't be seen, because they scared me.

Despite the fact I was feeling miserable that night, I remember that I had an innate sense humming inside me that indicated I was on the verge of a breakthrough. I had learned to listen to my instincts, so I shut my eyes for a moment, and when I opened them the first thing I saw was a sign tacked to my bulletin board. It had been there for years, and I had read it hundreds of times, but for reasons I'll never understand, in this moment, it seared into my mind and reached down to the base of my being. It was a Wayne Dyer quote that simply read: *Change your perspective and you will change your life.*

I decided to change my perspective by whirling around in my chair and found myself staring at my bookcase. The shelves were groaning under the weight of millions of words from hundreds of authors from across two millennia. A book of quotations caught my eye, so I opened it at random and it fell open to a page containing just the words I needed at that moment:

See the things that you want as already yours.
Know that they will come to you at need.
Then let them come. Don't fret and worry about
them. Don't think about your lack of them.
Think of them as yours, as belonging to you,
as already in your possession.
Robert Collier

That struck home. It was evident to me that my primary relationship to my finances was all about "fret and worry," and now this gentleman (whom, I now know, is a very famous New Thought leader who wrote those words long before I was born), had reached across the decades to tell me to alter my focus from fear to faith. A fundamental change swept over me, because I knew I had stumbled across a magnificent piece of wisdom. But I also knew from my past failures that this knowledge would be worthless without action.

I dug to the very back of the filing cabinet and filched out the file packed with bills, and began to write checks for each. I signed them and inserted the exact amount and the name of the payee, but I left the date blank.

Then I spread them out in front of me and spoke truth to power: "I'm not going to allow you to terrify me any longer. I know all of the money I need and more will eventually be earned. This is just a temporary setback; it is not the end. I am grateful to each bill because you represent many of the wonderful things in my life, such as our home, heat, food to eat, children to clothe, and a car to drive. I am a very fortunate person, privileged to live in an abundant universe, and I am grateful to my Creator for all the blessings in my life now, as well as those I know I will receive in the future."

I had changed my perspective ... and, so, I had changed my life. Over the next few months, all of those checks were eventually dated and paid in full. And now that I was no longer plagued by the doomsday scenarios that had been filling my mind, I was able to increase my productivity, secure in the knowledge that my life would be blessed beyond my wildest imaginings. I can tell you that Robert Collier's words are the truth. If you eliminate whatever is causing you doubt and anxiety in your life and follow the *Go 4 It!* plan, the same will occur for you.

Visual goal book

For me, pictures can speak louder than words, so I decided years ago that I would create my own visual goal book. It's very simple to do, and I suggest you give it a try. While it's important to have immediate goals, we also need to have longer-term goals. I continue to add to my visual goal book to this day, even though it's falling apart and I can only keep it together with rubber bands! I started work on it after returning from a weekend event with Tony Robbins, shortly after I had my first *Go 4 It!* moment.

All you need is a blank book, a glue stick, a pair of scissors, and the willingness to cut up your newspapers and magazines when you see something that catches your eye. While this is largely about the things money can buy, like houses, cruises and private jets, it is also a testimony to the splendor and abundance of the world, the places we can go, and the magnificence of the universe. So, dream big and don't forget to include topics such as generosity and a commitment to help others. (If you need a boost in that department, read the short biopics on the extraordinary people I've included at the end of this book.)

If you're an actor, cut out a picture of an Oscar

award. Or perhaps you plan to be number one (as I do) on the *New York Times* bestseller list, so cut out the bestseller list from this week's paper. Perhaps you're a chef and plan to open your own restaurant – go for it. Or you may want to operate your own health club.

In my case, goals having to do with health and fitness were important. I remember the day I read an article about the Ironman Triathlon (swim 2.4 miles, bike 112 miles, run 26.2 miles, without stopping). When I pasted the photo of their logo in my book, I had no idea how much work it would take to achieve that goal, but achieve it I did – not just once but twice!

This is a fun assignment, and it will be with you for the rest of your life, so give it a try.

Dreams + Action + Belief and Persistence = REALITY

CHAPTER 6

Speak Truth to Power

Courage is resistance to fears,
mastery of fear, not absence of fear.
Mark Twain

There are endless examples of people who have exhibited genuine bravery. Consider the boldness it must have taken for Rosa Parks to refuse to relinquish her seat on a bus to a white man in Montgomery, Alabama, in 1955. Today, this might appear to be a simple and safe act of defiance, but in the context of the Jim Crow era in the Deep South, Mrs. Parks knew her refusal could result in a bomb being thrown through her front door, or worse.

Instead, it launched the Montgomery Bus Boycott, which became a seminal moment in the history of the civil rights movement in America. When she was asked why she did it, her reply was that she was "simply tired of giving in." Rosa Parks spoke truth to power and changed the world in the process.

On February 20, 1962, John Glenn elected to stay in his seat inside the capsule of *Friendship 7*, despite eleven delays during countdown, and the knowledge that the mission had a one-in-six chance of failure. No stranger to risk, Glenn had flown 149 combat missions and, in 1957, set the transcontinental speed record.

When I speak with groups about the *Go 4 It!* approach to life, I am frequently astounded by the number of people who truly lust after the freedom and other rewards of this lifestyle but would like it to appear on their doorstep wrapped in a neat little box and stamped with a seal reading: *Absolutely Risk Free.*

Trust me, folks, that's not going to happen. But If you are willing to take on what feels like risk, and follow a few simple steps, everything can change. As an example, I love to tell this story about Howard, a young man in his late 20s, who stood up and asked this question at a *Go 4 It!* event:

"Bob, the one thing I know is that I hate my job and my boss. Every time he calls me into his office I think I'm going get fired, because he always complains about my work. The truth is that I feel sick to my stomach all day long.

"But when you asked us to think about what we wanted to do with our lives, and write it down as our Definite Decision, I didn't have any trouble coming up with an answer. I love to fly drones, and have become an expert at it. I teach all of my friends how to fly and I fix them for free, and everybody says I should turn this into a business. I think drones are the next big thing and I have this idea to open a shop, but what if I try it and I fail?"

The whole group talked it through for a few minutes, and Howard started to see that he was simply allowing his negative tapes (the "risk management team") to project failure and keep him in the rut he was in. He knew he was trading his freedom and self-respect and even admitted that it was fear that kept him trapped.

We debated the pros and cons of Howard's situation and the group voted on whether or not Howard should "Go for it." Everyone raised their hand, except for Howard. While the rest of us were chanting, "Go-for–it, Go–for–it," Howard shook his head, put his hands up and said, "I'm just not 100 percent certain."

About a year later, I was downtown, and noticed a storefront with a sign that read *Heavenly Drones*. I looked in the window, and sure enough, there was Howard, chatting with a customer. He was clearly excited and it was obvious from his animated style that he had become a new person. His body language shouted confidence.

I went inside and we high-fived, and I said, "Howard, you look like a new man!" I told him how happy I was that he had decided to make the leap and asked what had happened to change his mind.

"I just couldn't get the sound of everybody chanting out of my head. I brought all of my new friends home with me. It's almost like all those voices were drowning out my self-limiting beliefs. So a few days later I sat down at my kitchen table and started to develop a plan, and all of a sudden, it went from being scary to being an adventure. The more I worked on my plan, the more real it became.

"So, I made Heavenly Drones my Definite Decision. And soon, when I began to focus on it, it was all I could think about. I would sit down and picture this shop in my mind and it became real to me! I started to sketch out how it would look. I went to my computer and created a logo. Then I got serious and figured out how to get some small business loans, and started working from my kitchen table. A month later I finally quit my job, and last week we opened the shop!"

Howard was like a caged lion that had finally been released. Now, a year later, his shop is the go-to place for all things having to do with drones in the area.

To be honest, I still have vestiges of the same resistance in me, so it's time to tell on myself:

I was recently watching an episode of *Steve Austin's Broken Skull Challenge* with my three teenage sons when I casually mentioned I might just sign up to compete on the show. The next thing I knew, all three of them were rolling on the floor, imitating a decrepit old coot curled up in pain and begging for mercy at the first challenge on what is unquestionably a terrifying obstacle course. Well, that's all the incentive I needed to actually do it. I swore I would sign up the next day and show them that their old man's not a wimp.

However, when I visited the web page for applicants and viewed a few videos of the most dangerous and intimidating set of physical challenges imaginable, it soon became obvious the show was not interested in wasting their time with self-delusional crackpots; and Steve Austin's voice-over warning said as much. I decided to put Steve Austin out of my mind pretty quickly.

I wasn't going to get off so easily. Over the next few days, my boys had taken to regularly asking me some version of "So, hey, Dad, how's that sign-up at Skull Crusher Ranch going?"

To which I replied, "I'm getting there, don't you worry about it!"

But when I was alone with my wife, I asked her what she thought I should do. I mean, getting my skull crushed has never been on my bucket list.

"You think I should sign up? What if I don't have what it takes to even make it through the first round?"

So there it was; doubt had started to creep in, already crystallizing into fear and abject terror.

Kelly didn't even bother to look away from her magazine. "First of all, nobody cares; second, that's probably not going to happen if you take the time to prepare; and third, even if it did happen, what's the big deal?"

The honest answer to that last question was that I was afraid of being embarrassed. As far as I know, no one has ever actually "died of embarrassment." It's true that embarrassment *will* cause a bad feeling, but guess what? Bad feelings always pass, and they are usually just a product of our imagination.

I went to the website and signed up, and I have to admit that it's pretty intimidating to imagine yourself competing against some of the toughest hombres on the planet on an obstacle course that's designed to split your head open. The next day I received a polite reply informing me that I was on a waiting list. I took that to mean that I will soon be on the show, and immediately intensified my workouts so I'll be ready when I get the call.

Your personal self-investigation

The concept of speaking truth to power is generally attributed to a Quaker pamphlet dating back to the 1950s as an expression of their opposition to war. The phrase became popular over the years in association with historical moments when those who were being oppressed found the courage to stand up to their oppressors.

I've told you a bit of my story, so you know that I believe we all carry around our own personal oppressor. It is represented by our doubts and fears. No one likes to focus on things that scare them, so we avoid thinking about our fears. But that just gives them more power over us ... like the bills I hid, or my fear of being embarrassed at Skull Crusher Ranch, or Howard's willingness to continue to stay in a miserable job rather than live his dream.

Unless we consciously combat these thoughts, they will control our behaviors. So, I'm asking you now to start writing down some of your fears. In order to defeat your enemy, you must identify it, locate it and cut off its head. It's time to take out your sword (or at least your pen)!

MY TOP THREE FEARS

1. Not having enough money

2. Failing in my career

3. Not being loved or wanted by a romantic partner

WHY THEY SCARE ME

1. MAKES ME FEEL LIKE I'M NOT ENOUGH

2. PEOPLE WILL JUDGE ME

3. I WON'T BE ABLE TO HELP PEOPLE

HOW I WILL DEFEAT THEM

1.

2.

3.

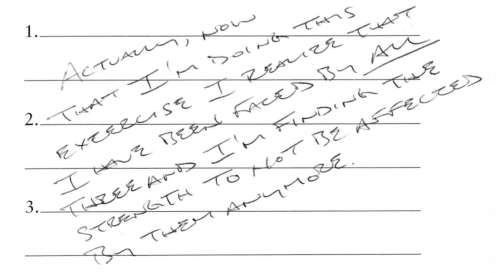

ACTUALLY, NOW THAT I'M DOING THIS EXERCISE I REALIZE THAT I HAVE BEEN FACED BY ALL THREE AND I'M FINDING THE STRENGTH TO NOT BE AFFECTED BY THEM ANYMORE.

Keep in mind that you may want to add to this list as time goes on. I suggest keeping a journal to track of your progress. Fears don't ever go away. The fears you have today, once defeated, will simply give way to new fears in the future, but you will be able to slay them one by one.

Let's also keep in mind that all your life, you have performed courageous acts simple things like attending the first day of school or having to give a speech, step up to the plate with bases loaded or stand up to a bully. It doesn't matter what happened in each of those situations. What matters is that you demonstrated courage. Give it some thought and record as many of these courageous acts as you like.

I AM COURAGEOUS

I HAVE DEALT WITH DEBT
COLLECTORS AND THE IRS MYSELF,
I HAVE BORROWED MONEY FROM
MY PARENTS, I HAVE FAILED
MANY TIMES IN MY CAREER AND
BOUNCED BACK, AND I HAVE BEEN
WITHOUT A RELATIONSHIP FOR 3 YEARS
AND A MORE THAN OK.

*I learned that courage was not the absence
of fear, but the triumph over it. The brave
man is not he who does not feel afraid,
but he who conquers that fear.*
Nelson Mandela

The quote above by Nelson Mandela really says it
all, and he was certainly someone who knew something about courage, not to mention patience.

I'd like to end this chapter by trying to put the
whole topic of fears and courage into perspective.
Obviously, there are real fears and imagined fears,
and it would be foolhardy to ignore reality and jump
into something that scares you, without first developing a plan.

Howard's approach is a perfect example. He sat
down at his kitchen table and started to write a business plan, and as he did, he came up with answers to
each of his obstacles. He didn't allow the "What if"
questions to stop him; instead he anticipated problems and found solutions, but accepted that he would
also need a strong dose of faith in order to succeed.
Ultimately, his vision allowed his new business to become real to him before it actually existed. That's the

Law of Abundance at work.

Learn to embrace the adventure of not being able to anticipate every issue. To be sure, Howard has encountered some difficult days, but he has succeeded because he embraced the *Go 4 It!* attitude. When he walks out his front door each morning, he knows he will have challenges and that he will overcome them. And, in case he ever utters something like "Why did I ever open this store?" he has a little personal leverage, in the form of the photo of his old boss tacked on the wall!

CHAPTER 7

Money and the Behavioral Landmines to Avoid

Author's note to the next two chapters:

So, now, that we've covered the whole topic of fear, let's talk about the subject that never fails to turn on the emotional juices … MONEY.

I don't care who you are – it's pretty safe to say that you want more money. Many people (including me at one point) struggle in their relationship with money, and this HAS to be addressed and resolved before you can really begin earning the money you desire for your life.

This whole aspect of one's relationship to money is covered in much greater context in my book, *"Get Tough, Retire Rich!"* I also offer short weekly "Energizer" videos that help subscribers all over the world get a handle on their energy around the subject of money and learn to direct that energy in a truly powerful, positive path.

For *this* book, though – and your new *"Go 4 It!"* decision and action – I wanted to offer a couple chapters on building a sound investment portfolio by way of bulleted, fast-track points of advice.

In my opinion, there's no one better in the world for this sort of advice than my business partner, Peter.

I've already mentioned by business partner, Peter Mallouk, in these pages. Peter is one of the most respected financial advisors in the county. You might see him on Tony Robbins stage, co-writing books with Tony Robbins, and appearing on an endless number of financial news shows. Analysts and commentators consistently seek out Peter's perspective on the ever-changing, somewhat volatile markets of the day.

I count myself extremely fortunate to work daily with Peter, and consider him my closest friend. He's taking over the wheel here for these next two chapters – I know you're in for a most adventurous and educational ride.

– BP

Most people who get excited about investing dive into research, read market timing or stock pick letters, use online services, and watch financial news all the time. The idea is that the more they know, the better informed they will become and the less likely they will make a mistake.

It doesn't really work this way.

If you have a reasonable level of intelligence and you understand the basic principles of investing, you will likely outperform the great majority of investors.

The key is to not mess things up. Easy, right?

Unfortunately, there are plenty of ways to do just that.

While I'll be addressing a few basic rules of thumb in the next chapter, I want to start here with how your behavior can cause significant havoc in your portfolio.

There is nothing I have personally seen cause more financial destruction than the emotionally driven mistakes investors make. The key is to recognize your behavioral biases so that you can knowingly protect yourself from making mistakes. Let's dive in.

Fear, Greed, and Herding

As humans, fear and greed are two of our ugliest

85

traits and most powerful forces. They can impact the way we live our lives, and they can have very negative consequences for investors. Novice investors fall prey to it, legendary investors know how to control it, and the media and market prognosticators feed into it.

Fear and greed, combined with our natural bias toward herding, can cause major investment mistakes. Humans are hardwired to move in herds, to follow the crowd, and to find safety in consensus. If the market is going down and the media, commentators, and our friends are yelling "head for the exits," our herding instinct, coupled with the powerful force of fear, is to do the same. If the market is rallying, and everyone is saying "full steam ahead," our herding instinct, coupled with the alluring force of greed, entices us to join the crowd. The herding instinct can be very costly.

Unfortunately, these instincts can cause the investor irreparable damage. In bear markets, a more sophisticated investor is better served to take the opportunity to buy more. This is often referred to as opportunistic rebalancing. During substantial market drops, the smart investor is selling off bonds and buying stocks. With patience, this strategy has put the investor in a better place, every time. Warren Buffett has historically held his positions and aggressively added during periods of investor hysteria. He has said to "be fearful when others are greedy and greedy when others are fearful."

In a 2014 interview, former Federal Reserve Chairman Alan Greenspan reflected back on all he had learned. Interestingly, rather than lots of economic analysis, he shared his observations of human behavior saying:

If you can grit your teeth through and just disregard short-term declines in the market or even long-term declines in the market, you will come out well. I mean you just stick all your money in stocks and go home and don't look at your portfolio you'll do far better than if you try to trade it. The reason that's the case is this asymmetry between fear and euphoria.* The most successful stock market players, the best investors, are those who recognize that the asymmetric bias in fear vs. euphoria is a tradable concept and can't fail for precisely this reason. (Fox 2014)

That's some pretty interesting insight from the

person most people considered the most powerful person on earth for much of his tenure.Control your fear, control your greed, avoid the herd, and things will work out.

The Overconfidence Effect

The overconfidence effect is a well-established bias in which someone's personal confidence in their judgments is greater than reality, especially when confidence is relatively high. Let's be clear though; there's nothing wrong with confidence.

Confidence is simply trusting your abilities. Your mom wants you to be confident, your coach wants you to be confident, and I want you to be confident. Overconfidence, though, is quite dangerous as it means you are overestimating your ability to get something right. This can result in some rather poor decision making in life and investing.

In his book, *The Psychology of Judgment and Decision Making*, Scott Plous said, "No problem in judgment and decision making is more prevalent and more potentially catastrophic than overconfidence" (Plous 1993, 217). It has been blamed for lawsuits, strikes, wars, and stock market bubbles and crashes.

No, he isn't exaggerating.

The overconfidence effect has been studied and documented in the investment world more than any other area. Finance professors Brad Barber and Terrance Odean examined the trading patterns of 35,000 households over a five- year period. They found that men's overconfidence in their abilities resulted in 45 percent more trading activity than women. And what exactly did all of this overconfidence get them? The trading *reduced* their average return by 2.65 percent per year, far underperforming the women. On top of that, the men paid more in transaction fees and taxes. Overconfidence can be very expensive.

In another study, a researcher found that when analysts are 80 percent certain a stock will go up, they are right just 40 percent of the time (Van Eaton 2000).

This is quite similar to the impact of additional information on investing. We know that those who gather more information feel better about their investments and trade more, and we know that those who trade more underperform more. These investors are mistaking all of the additional information they are collecting as added intelligence that will enable them to trade to their advantage.

Instead, the studies bear out that the added information results in overconfidence which, in turn, results in activity in the account that is actually a waste of a bunch of time, money, effort and stress – all to create underperformance.

When you hear someone make a big, bold market prediction, it is usually accompanied by a large dose of overconfidence. There are simply too many variables to predict short-term market movements, and anyone knowledgeable about markets would never make a bold short-term prediction. The bolder the call, the less valid the opinion.

Confirmation Bias

Confirmation bias is the tendency for people to look for and favor information that confirms their preconceptions and beliefs and to avoid, devalue or dismiss information that conflicts with their beliefs.

For example, a conservative may read the *Wall Street Journal,* view the Drudge Report online, and watch FOX News, while a liberal may read the *New York Times,* view the *Huffington Post* online, and watch MSNBC. Both are seeking out information that usually confirms their ideas and are avoiding information that may conflict with their ideas.

When was the last time you subscribed to a magazine, bought a book, or regularly listened to or watched a political pundit who challenged your views? If you are like most people, it's been a long time. In fact, you probably spend most of your time validating what you think is right.

You see, we all think we are right – and not just about some important things, about everything! And we constantly seek ways to validate what we think. *Highly intelligent people are doing just the opposite and instead are actively seeking out opposing views, challenging their ideas, and even occasionally changing their minds.*

Even Warren Buffett said that he finds himself falling prey to confirmation bias and actively seeks out other investors who disagree staunchly with his ideas.

One way to deal with confirmation bias is to ask yourself everything that can go wrong. For example, if you really like the idea of investing in a specific investment, pretend 10 years has passed and that you have lost a substantial sum of money on it. Ask yourself all the ways that might have happened. This forces your brain to go through the exercise of acknowledging or even, dare I say, welcoming adverse ideas.

Anchoring

Anchoring is a term psychologists use to explain the way the brain takes mental shortcuts to arrive at conclusions. In short, there is a tendency for us to over-rely on the first piece of information that enters our brain. This piece of information is the "anchor." Once the anchor is set, all future decisions revolve around the anchor, contaminating rational thinking. If you are ever not certain of a correct answer, most likely you will fall victim to the anchoring bias and guess an answer based on the most recent information.

Anchoring is well known by both novice and experienced negotiators. The first price thrown out in a negotiation often becomes the anchor.

The anchoring effect with stock purchases is often – you guessed it – your purchase price. If you purchase a stock for $50 and it is later $30, you may hold onto it until it gets back to $50, or even buy more because you think it is worth $50. If instead the stock goes from $50 to $70, you may sell the stock thinking it is overvalued because the price is so much higher than $50. Your decision making is clouded by your anchor.

Many investors fall victim to anchoring by buying a stock that has come far off its highs ("It's a bargain now!"), or not purchase a stock that has run on to new highs ("It is too overpriced now!").

The only reason the investor thinks it is a great bargain or overpriced is because of the direction it has moved from its past "anchor" price. With a heightened sense of awareness of the anchoring bias, you can avoid holding losers too long and selling winners too early.

Loss Aversion

Quite simply, loss aversion is the bias humans have to avoid a loss rather than make a gain. In other words, we fear losing more than we enjoy winning. Losses hurt more than the pleasure we get from gains.

Loss aversion is the reason that you hang on to a stock long after it has dropped. You don't want to acknowledge the loss, which would require you to no longer deny you made a mistake. Far better to just wait until it (maybe) recovers, right?

Whenever I am talking with a client who has an investment they won't sell until it recovers, I ask them a simple question: "If you had cash instead of this stock, knowing what you are trying to accomplish, would you buy the same stock today?" The answer is almost always no, and when it is, we know the investor is hanging on only because of the loss aversion effect.

Mental Accounting

Psychologist Hal Arkes' research shows us that mental accounting is the reason tax refunds and lottery winnings are often blown quickly (Arkes et al. 1994). Mental accounting puts them in the "free money" column. We all know a dollar is really just a dollar though!

If you have ever gambled and found yourself winning, you may notice you became more aggressive when you were playing with "house money." Again, the mental accounting effect is at work. Money is money; we just account for it differently because of our human biases. Mental accounting impacts the way we make decisions in everyday life, and is a contributor to wealth destruction among investors who

94

fall into its trap.

If an investor looks at each individual investment separately, this results in creating separate mental accounts for each holding. By doing this, the investor is far more likely to hold onto losers in any account with a loss than to wait for it to break even, and to sell off winners in the accounts with gains to "lock it in."

Looking at each holding or subaccount piecemeal can result in mental accounting that can trigger poor decision making. If you hold separate investment accounts, keep in mind they should not be judged individually, but rather as to whether they contribute appropriately to your long-term objective. By looking at the "big picture," it is far easier to judge if you are on track for your long- term goals.

Recency Bias

Recency bias is the tendency to project one's most recent experiences or observations into the future. This mental shortcut lets us make predictions about what will happen in the future based on what happened in the recent past. The problem is, this mental shortcut can create lots of problems for investors.

Studies show brokers tend to recommend hot stocks that have outperformed over the previous year, but that those recommendations underperform the market in the following year. Investors tend to jump on stocks that have risen many months in a row, expecting the trend to continue.

The market went down almost constantly in late 2008 and 2009, causing many investors to expect the recent events to continue. Exiting the market, the investors missed out on the inevitable recovery. Whenever the market appears calm and rises steadily, money pours in from the sidelines, eager to buy once things appear stable.

Of course, markets don't work like this. In any given year, the odds are high the market will end the year positive, regardless of what happened the year before. In any given year, the odds are good there will be a correction, regardless of what happened the prior weeks, months, or years. In any given decade, an investor can expect about two bear markets, regardless of what happened the previous decade.

One effective tool to combat recency bias in investing is to follow a disciplined system for managing your money. For example, if you are in a portfolio of 70 percent stocks and 30 percent bonds, you might decide to rebalance only when the allocation changes by more than 5 percent. Another system is to set trades according to a calendar. With a system like this, your investment decisions will be based on your disciplined process rather than on recent market events.

Negativity Bias

Negativity bias is the nature of humans to recall negative experiences more vividly than positive ones, and therefore act consciously and subconsciously to avoid negative experiences.

The negativity bias certainly helped humans survive thousands of years ago. It made sense to constantly look around for potential things that could kill you – you know, things like wild animals, crazy people with spears, and the like. Today, the negativity bias is a dead weight dragging the unsuspecting down.

The negativity bias is well at work in the investment world. We know that investors feel the pain of losses twice as much as the pleasure of gains. This tilt toward the negative encourages investors suffering from negativity bias to sell during corrections—at precisely the wrong time. They would rather run to cash than experience the pain of the negative experience.

As with all behavioral biases, the best way to combat it is to be aware of it, recognize it, and squash it before the negativity bias negatively impacts you or your portfolio.

The Gambler

We all have a subconscious desire to gamble. That's why Las Vegas always finds a way to make money. Human psychology is such that if we are winning, our endorphins go crazy, and we keep playing because it feels good. Human psychology also encourages us to keep playing when we are losing. We keep playing for two reasons: We want to feel good again, but also because we hate losing and desperately want to break even.

Casinos know this, of course.

Our human biases encourage us to keep playing, whether we are winning or losing, which makes sure the house odds ultimately work out for the casino. The odds of winning a hand at blackjack are around 49 percent. A casino can't stay in business if people bet a hand of blackjack once or twice. The casino would lose about half the time. But, if you play a few hundred hands of blackjack, the odds are overwhelmingly against you. When was the last time you played one or two hands of blackjack, or any casino game?

The market is just as unforgiving. While the market itself goes up, the stocks within it can move all over the place, and as we know, most of the stocks underperform the market. Trading stocks also has a "house" or two that win every time: the brokerage house, which will collect a commission and the IRS, which will collect taxes. The odds that an investor will win trading stocks is the same as that of a gambler winning at the tables in Las Vegas, less than 50 percent. And as with gambling, the more times an investor trades, the more likely the odds will catch up with him and he will lose.

Have you ever noticed what your online trading platform looks and sounds like? It's green and red, with scrolling tickers, flashing images, and dinging sounds. Just like a casino. Do you think that is a coincidence?

Conclusion to Behavioral Traps

Ultimately, it is our own behavior that does us in. The key to dodging this pitfall is to be aware of what your instincts are telling you and recognize the behavioral landmines we have covered in this chapter. Take a step back, slow down, and follow the disciplined plan you have laid out for you and your family. The car is going to get to its destination, unless you personally drive it off the cliff.

CHAPTER 8
Getting Investing Right

When it comes to investing, much of the game is simply not messing things up. We have covered that in detail thus far. But, of course, the goal is to not only avoid getting in the way of success; it is to maximize the odds of success.

Having gone over the key mistakes to avoid, let's discuss how to optimize your results.

Rule #1 – Have a Clearly Defined Plan

You don't start a race without knowing where the finish line is. You don't go on a hike without knowing your destination and the conditions you may encounter. You don't start driving somewhere without knowing where you are going. Nonetheless, most investors invest without an endgame laid out in advance. Without a destination, it is easy to drift off course. Without a plan, it is easy to change the strategy midstream, increasing the odds of messing everything up.

Before you invest one dollar, you must have a plan. A plan does not need to be a 150-page road map of how you will invest every minute for the rest of your life. A plan can be very straightforward.

Step 1 — We simply begin with determining the starting line, which is where you are today. Build a net worth statement that lays out all of your assets and liabilities.

Step 2 — Then, you need to know your goal. A goal must be very specific and realistic. An example of a goal that would not work well is: "I want to retire with a lot of money." Come on, people! We need to have a clearly defined purpose. Something like this will work: "I would like to retire at age 62 with a post-tax income of $100,000 per year adjusted for inflation, and I want to assume social security will not be there for me." Now that is something we can work with!

Step 3 — Run a projection showing how on track you are for that goal. There are online tools to help you do this, or your advisor can do this with you. Be sure to exclude assets that are not available to fund retirement. Start with the money you have today that is available for retirement, which is $650,000 ($800,000 less the $150,000 you need for the kids). Then, include the money you are saving regularly, whether it is to your retirement plan at work, an IRA, or a taxable account. It is here that we will determine how on track you may be for your goals.

Step 4 — Now, determine if you need to adjust your goal. For example, if your projection shows that to hit your goal you need to have an investment rate of return of 20 percent a year, well, change the goal, because it very likely isn't going to work out. You can adjust your goal by lowering your income need, saving more, or pushing your retirement date out.

Step 5 — Once we have a starting point and an end goal, we can move on to building the portfolio. Note that your plan needs to be revisited regularly (more on this later).

Rule #2 – Avoid Asset Classes That Diminish Results

There are five major asset classes: cash, commodities (like gold and energy), stocks, bonds, and real estate. Here, I'm primarily addressing the two asset classes that should never be included in an investor's portfolio, and then I'll cover how to construct an allocation targeted toward your goals.

Cash – The Illusion of Safety

First and foremost, cash is the worst performing asset class in history. Over long periods of time, cash has always underperformed all other major asset classes. The more time you spend with a significant portion of your holdings in cash, the higher the probability your portfolio will underperform.

Second, holding cash for long periods of time guarantees that you will not keep up with inflation. Cash guarantees the loss of purchasing power. In essence, your cash becomes worth less and less each year as prices go up and your cash does not.

One reason many "investors" hold cash is to time

the market. They do this despite the fact that there has never been a documented, real-world study done by anyone ever showing that repeatedly moving from the market to cash and back to the market works.

Finally, many investors hold cash in the event of financial Armageddon, a situation when the stock market goes to zero or near zero and never recovers. In reality, if we live in a world where Walmart, Nike, McDonald's, Exxon Mobil, and the rest of the world's dominant companies go down and never recover, it will likely accompany a default by the U.S. government on treasury bonds.

How can the U.S. government make its debt payments on its bonds if the major U.S. companies have collapsed? Who exactly would be working and paying taxes to cover the debt payments? In this event, cash is worthless as the FDIC guarantee would essentially mean nothing. If you do not believe America's major corporations can survive, then the natural conclusion is that the U.S. economic system itself cannot survive. In that event, cash may be the worst asset to own.

While cash brings comfort, it does not keep up with inflation, constantly loses purchasing power, drags down long-term investment returns, and is of no value in the event of a true economic collapse. Keeping short-term reserves on hand is a good idea. Hoarding cash as a long-term investment, not so much.

The Illusion of Gold as a Way to Grow Wealth

Many investors are flocking to gold as they worry that the dollar is losing so much value it may become worthless. Others worry the global economy will collapse, and gold will be the one true currency. Unlike companies, real estate, and energy, gold itself is nearly intrinsically worthless. Companies and real estate have the potential to create income. Energy companies have the potential to produce income. Oil itself is used as one of the most critical resources in the global economy. Gold produces no income and is not a critical resource.

Historically, gold has performed worse than stocks, real estate, energy, and bonds, barely keeping pace with inflation (see Figure 6.1). Every time in history it has outperformed substantially, it has ultimately collapsed.

If you own gold in your portfolio, expect to not get paid an income, pay higher taxes on your returns, take a more volatile ride than the stock market, and get a long-term return lower than bonds. No thanks.

Rule #3 – Use Stocks and Bonds as the Core

Building Blocks of Your Intelligently Constructed Portfolio

Bonds

Bonds deliver a positive return about 85 percent of the time. With a bond you are loaning money to a company or other entity.

- A treasury bond is a loan to the federal government.
- A municipal bond is a loan to a municipality such as a city or state.
- A corporate bond is a loan to a corporation like McDonald's or Nike.
- A high yield bond, also known as a junk bond, is a loan to a corporation that has to pay higher interest to attract investors to loan them money.

A lender is in a more predictable position than a stockholder. As long as the company stays around, the lender gets paid back with interest, while a stockholder never really knows what will happen as the stock can fluctuate all over the place. *It is for this reason that, over the long run, bonds are expected to underperform stocks. You should not own bonds on the expectation they will do otherwise.*

So, if bonds are expected to underperform, why in the world might you buy them? First, while stocks are very likely to perform well over 10 years, there is a lot of precedent for prolonged periods of misery (see 9/11, the tech bubble, or 2008/2009 for a modern-day refresher). It is important that income needs be met for three to seven years so that the investor is never at the mercy of the stock market's often random gyrations. That way, between the bonds and their income, you can get the monthly income you need.

Basically, bonds are insurance. *We are giving up expected return in exchange for dramatically increasing the likelihood the investor's needs will be met in the short and long run.*

Stocks

Stocks are the subject of ceaseless predictions, when really they are the most unpredictable and predictable (yes, both) asset class. No one, absolutely no one, can predict the short-term movement of stock prices.

Because stocks are not predictable in the short run, an investor should not own them to meet short-term needs. However, over the long run, stocks are expected to perform far better than bonds. Because stocks are riskier than bonds, they come with an implied "risk premium." If bonds were expected to perform as well, no one would ever take on the volatility that comes with owning stocks.

While this inevitable outcome has persisted for over a century, the constant corrections, crashes, and day-to-day movements drive out the fainthearted or cause them to jump ship at the worst possible time.

Part of having the patience to make it through all this is to have stock market exposure only for the portion of your portfolio allocated for income needs more than five years out, depending on a variety of factors. If you are not at the mercy of the market over the next few years, and we know over the long run the market has done nothing but go up, it becomes far easier to get through the rollercoaster ride along the way.

Real Estate, Energy, and MLPs

For higher-net-worth investors, adding real estate and energy can serve as inflation hedges. The best way to buy real estate is using an indexed ETF or index fund. The best way to gain exposure to energy is by owning an energy company index ETF or index fund. Avoid holdings that own oil itself. These track the price of oil and the return can vary widely from the actual price of oil.

Rule #4 – Take a Global Approach

Investors tend to have a home country bias, meaning they invest most of their money in companies that operate in their home country. This is evidenced all over the world.

Nonetheless, U.S. investors should use international holdings as part of their portfolio for several reasons:

1. We live in a global economy and companies everywhere can and do make money;
2. International holdings often behave somewhat differently than U.S. holdings;
3. The U.S. markets and international markets often "take turns" out performing one another for short and sometimes long periods of time;
4. The difference in returns can dampen portfolio

volatility; and

5. Many international economies, especially the emerging market economies, have far higher projected growth rates than the United States.

One does not need to become an international exchange expert to create a global portfolio. By simply purchasing an index fund, an investor can instantly add global exposure.

Rule #5 – Use Primarily Index-Based Positions

Actively trading securities in any asset class will likely yield lower returns. Choose index-based holdings for most – if not all – of your portfolio.

Rule #6 – Don't Blow Out Your Existing Holdings

Once you have determined the right allocation for you, work toward it as quickly as possible. Any investments in tax-deferred accounts like 401(k)s, 403(b)s, IRAs, and the like can immediately be sold and repositioned. Any new money you add to the portfolio can be placed into the new investments as well.

However, resist the temptation to sell all the holdings in your taxable account. While it is true that the

S&P 500 will likely outperform the large company stocks you currently own, it very likely may not outperform on an after-tax basis.

The goal is to get as close as possible to the target portfolio without creating a tax hit that likely cannot be overcome. Yes, the S&P 500 may do better, but likely not by enough to cover the tax hit.

With customization, the portfolio can yield a far better after-tax result.

Rule #7 – Asset Location Matters

Taxes matter. They matter a lot. Advisors don't talk about it much because if you knew the tax bill they generated with all of their trading, you would fire them. The same goes for mutual funds, hedge funds, and the like.

For example, let's say you have an investment manager who actively trades your $1 million account. At the end of the year, you get a report saying you earned 7 percent, or $70,000. You are a pretty happy camper. A few months later, you will receive a 1099 and possibly other reports to be used for your tax preparation. If you are like most people, you will never look at it, throw it in a folder, and once all your stuff is together, you will give it to your CPA.

Now, let's say that the report shows that you owe taxes of $30,000. This will be blended in with the rest of your taxes, and if your CPA asks you to cut a check to pay the IRS, you will. The $30,000 will probably not be paid out of your investment account, and even if it is, the report will forever show your rate of return was 7 percent, when in fact it was 4 percent after taxes.

Asset location can mitigate much of the damage. When building out your portfolio, resist the temptation to make every account look the same. Instead, place the investments that create substantial taxes into your tax deferred accounts. For example, put your taxable bonds and real estate investments in your IRA or 401(k). Place the investments that do not create a lot of taxes, like large company stocks, in your taxable account. By simply purchasing assets in the most tax-efficient location possible, you will improve your after-tax return.

Rule #8 – Be Sure You Can Live with Your Allocation

I have three kids—two are 8 years old and one is 13. Whenever we go to the amusement park, they examine the various roller coasters. Even kids attempt to make decisions as to the sort of ride they can handle.

In the past, I used to go on whatever roller coaster they wanted. In recent years, I have often found that to be a regretful decision, particularly during the slow climb up some ridiculously high hill and the near vomit-inducing drop. Even then, though, I realize that getting off the roller coaster and back on it in the middle of the ride is not a good idea. In fact, the odds are very good I will come out on the other end in one piece if I just follow it through to the end.

The markets are the same.

The bond market is much like the kiddie coaster at Lego Land. Almost anyone can handle it. The stock market is much like a big-time roller coaster at Six Flags. The real estate market is like Space Mountain at Disney World: fast and in the dark. The commodity market is more like the Detonator: a ride that drops and lifts you unpredictably.

All of these rides have various levels of speed and volatility. Some find them thrilling; others find them nauseating. But in all cases, the rides generally reach a peaceful conclusion, even to the passengers who are wondering exactly what they just got themselves into.

The best time to evaluate the roller coaster you are on is when the market is relatively stable. It is much easier to make that decision then, before the ride starts up again.

This is easier said than done. Americans are great at forgetting things. It is a great coping mechanism that allows us to move on. After going on a roller coaster with my son, I tell myself I won't do it again. But the next time I am at the amusement park with him, I agree to the stomach-dropping ride, not totally remembering how bad it actually felt the last time.

Smart investors customize their roller coaster, taking parts of various markets to build a portfolio that meets their short-, intermediate-, and long-term needs. A portfolio can twist and turn, taking on the volatility necessary to meet the investor's specific goals, but should be structured within the parameters that the investor is prepared to handle.

For many, the best portfolio is a portfolio that accomplished the intended goals with the least volatility possible. However, if the volatility is outside your bandwidth of tolerance, it is far better to adjust the goal or your savings plan than to make a mistake at the worst possible time.

Rule #9 – Revisit the Plan

Revisit your plan and projections once a year or any time a major change in your life happens. At your review, you will notice that your starting point may have changed. Your portfolio likely performed better or worse than expected over the previous year. You may have received an unexpected bonus, an inheritance, or had a liquidity event (for example, the sale of a property). The starting line has changed.

All sorts of things can change that should result in changes to the portfolio. Note that the emphasis on changes to the portfolio should be based far more on personal changes than changes in various markets.

The Ultimate Rule – Don't Mess It Up!

Once you have the portfolio in place, *stay disciplined*. Follow the pattern of investment decisions outlined in this chapter or work with an advisor who understands, accepts and invests with these principles. Ignore the noise, never panic, don't change plans in the middle of a crisis, and stay focused on your goals.

CHAPTER 9

When the Going Gets Tough—And It Will!

The brick walls are there for a reason. The brick walls are not there to keep us out. The brick walls are there to give us a chance to show how badly we want something. Because the brick walls are there to stop people who don't want it badly enough. They're there to stop the other people.

Randy Pausch, *The Last Lecture*

In 2007 there was a tremendous amount of attention in the media regarding a YouTube video and bestselling book called *The Last Lecture*. It was one of those things that went viral and literally took the world by storm because it was so enthralling. Here's the story:

Randy Pausch was a computer science professor at Carnegie Mellon University in Pittsburgh and a successful entrepreneur. Unfortunately, he was diagnosed with pancreatic cancer when he was only 45. A year later, he was told that he had between "three and six months of good health left" and that he would certainly be gone within a year.

Awful news for anyone, to be sure, but particularly for such an accomplished man with a wife and three young children. But Randy didn't just curl up and die; he made the most of his remaining time on earth.

On September 18, 2007, Professor Pausch gave a riveting "Last Lecture" address to his students, and the YouTube video went viral. It wasn't long before he was sitting opposite Oprah Winfrey, and then he co-authored a book that hit the top of the bestseller list a few months before he died on July 25, 2008.

At the time he gave his lecture, Randy looked to be in pretty good health, so much so that, at one point, he dropped to the floor and did several push-ups, to the astonishment of the crowd.

Here was a seemingly healthy man who knew he was going to die soon, yet he was determined to make one last attempt to leave something of enduring value for his children and the world. If you haven't heard the lecture or read the book, I suggest you do both, because (aside from beautifully reinforcing the importance of treating others with respect and the importance of love and forgiveness), it hammers home the point that there is an urgency to life that we cannot see but, nonetheless, is real and present.

Make friends with your brick walls

I selected the above quote to open this chapter because it perfectly sums up the mental toughness you will need to develop and sustain in order to reach whatever goals you have set. Make no mistake about it, there are forces out there than can trip you up.

A *Go 4 It!* lifestyle is for realists, and those of us who embrace it will welcome life's challenges, because we know those brick walls are actually our loving teachers.

Randy Pausch noted that life has a way of weeding out those who cannot break through the brick walls. Perhaps this has something to do with why so many people choose to live in a fantasy world. Consider this: Americans spend 192 million dollars on lottery tickets every day; despite the fact that the odds of winning the Powerball Lottery are only 1 in 175 million!

We are also influenced by friends, relatives and associates who delude themselves into believing that they will discover a secret door to fast and easy success. Granted, success is definitely going to come at an easier pace when you've made a Definite Decision and are taking action daily toward your envisioned end result, but you know as well as I do that this type of intentional success is an entirely different energy than the "quick fix" success solution you see coming at you from every turn.

I mentioned this before, but it is so important that it bears another mention: In order for you to sustain a *Go 4 It!* life over the long haul, you must be vigilant about the company you keep.

If your out-of-shape buddy tells you he plans to run a marathon next year and then announces he doesn't need to train on rainy mornings, do you believe he is really going to make it to the finish line? And isn't it interesting that the woman at your office who is constantly angry and has been threatening to quit for years is still glued to her seat, fiercely protecting her turf? We all know such people. They're the buzzards who will always tell you why something can't be done or why it won't go your way.

Instead, grow your own wings and take flight from the buzzards. Volunteer to do the impossible. So what if your first attempt fails? Simply change course and figure it out. But whatever you do, don't hang with the buzzards. (After all, their job is to chew on your carcass!)

My brick wall

Right about the time I was down in my basement, dead broke and lining up my invoices to pay them at some point in the future, I came across an ad for the Ironman Triathlon. I cut it out and glued it into my visual goal book, and then turned out the lights and went up to bed, thinking, "Someday, I'm definitely going to do that."

Once I was in bed, it dawned on me that competing in the most challenging physical contest on the planet wasn't a "someday" plan – it was a "today" plan.

I was about 40 at the time and, while I was in excellent shape, I knew it was going to take a year of intense conditioning to reach the point where I would be able to swim 2.4 miles, bike 112 miles, and run 26.2 miles (in that order) on a single day without a break in between. Think about it. That's twelve to fourteen hours without stopping for a break!

I had competed in half triathlons in my local area, but Ironman is the mother of all triathlons, and I knew I didn't have a minute to waste. Time was definitely not on my side.

So, the very next day, by the time I arrived at the gym I had devised a strategy for ramping up my exercise program each day. I knew that I needed to make continuous improvement if I was going to be able to reach my goal of competing within a year.

However, that meant that in addition to my ramped-up weekday workouts, I would have to devote roughly six hours on both Saturday and Sunday, regardless of whether it was freezing cold or blisteringly hot. There were times at the end of my swimming, riding, and running regimen when I would walk through the door and fall directly into an ice bath because every muscle in my body ached terribly.

Swimming was the worst. I was an adequate

swimmer, but I really couldn't stand jumping into a pool at 6:00 in the morning. I had promised myself, though, that I would swim at least three days per week. At the outset it was discouraging, because there were some excellent swimmers already in the pool at that ungodly hour of the morning, and I felt like I was paddling around like a rookie. But, little by little, I improved until eventually I was turning laps with the best of them.

Interestingly, the mental part of the event was the most difficult, and not just because of the pain and exhaustion in each of the events – I could handle that – but because I had a not-unreasonable fear of drowning. This was reinforced when I learned that when people perish while competing in all manner of triathlons throughout the world (and they do), in most cases it is due to drowning.

I had recently joined Creative Planning at the time I embarked on this adventure, and, unbeknownst to me, it would be several years before I turned the corner financially. So, in retrospect, I can see that I was using the triathlon as an allegory to demonstrate to myself that, through hard work and perseverance, I could accomplish the impossible. I planned to use this as leverage on myself. By pushing myself to the limit physically, I would reinforce my belief that I could apply the same mental toughness to achieve my financial goals.

When the day of the Ironman Triathlon arrived, I was ready. Of course, there were butterflies in my belly and my heart was thumping with excitement, but I was determined.

While the top athletes in this competition are shooting to win, the vast majority of us are really competing with ourselves. After all, this is the single hardest one-day physical challenge in the world. My goal was to finish the race within the allotted time, despite the tremendous pain my body was going to have to endure.

At the end of the last event, the marathon, I glanced over my shoulder just before I crossed the finish line and was elated to see hundreds of runners behind me. I had done it! In a few seconds, I fell to the ground and was overcome with a complex of emotions that unleashed tears of joy, relief and exhaustion.

The next year I had a very specific goal, which was to beat my time from the previous year, and I did. The instant I crossed that finish line, I knew I would never compete in another triathlon because I had proven my point to myself.

What is your *Go 4 It!* physical challenge?

The connection between physical and mental stamina is well established. Wherever you are in your life physically, there is always room for improvement. I challenge you to challenge yourself to improve. If you are a walker or a runner, do it faster and longer. Whatever your choice of exercise, you know that you can push yourself to greater heights. Do it. Stop making excuses. Begin to monitor your progress.

If you are a sedentary person, it's time to get moving, period. Perhaps you can only walk around the block. If that's all you can do, then do it. Tomorrow, take 100 additional steps, and 100 more the next day. I can guarantee you that it will start to change your attitude about yourself.

Whatever your primary *Go 4 It!* goal is, your chances of success will increase once you begin to focus on daily continuous improvement physically – because the physical is all mental, my friend – but the changes you will see physically reward you in a relatively faster way. And, when you feel better about your physical self, you're going to feel more energy, stamina and confidence in accomplishing steps and tasks that require perseverance and commitment to "break on through to the other side."

Of course, I'm proud of my Ironman experience, and it has certainly helped me in all areas of my life. Whenever I start to doubt myself, I use that experience as positive leverage, and tell myself something along the lines of: "Come on, Bob, you completed the Ironman Triathlon, not once but twice. This is going to be a piece of cake." By challenging ourselves and succeeding, we reinforce our belief in our ability to accomplish our future goals.

Persistence and unwillingness to give up mean that you must not relent, even when problems are dumped on you. Whining and worrying will only exacerbate the problem. In fact, those are precisely the moments when you must reach into your toolkit and rely upon the perseverance muscle you have developed.

When the Going Gets Tough—And It Will!

Take a minute to jot down your plan for how you will develop your perseverance muscle:

I WILL MAKE IT TO THE
GYM AT LEAST 4 DAYS
EVERY WEEK. REGARDLESS OF
HOW I FEEL. AND I WILL
ENGAGE IN PHYSICAL ACTIVITY OF
SOME SORT 7 DAYS A WEEK.

You may encounter many defeats,
but you must not be defeated. In fact,
it may be necessary to encounter the defeats, so you
can know who you are, what you can rise from,
how you can still come out of it.
Maya Angelou

The next time you are in a tough spot, take a deep breath and bring to mind the story of Vinny Paz.

The Pazmanian Devil

Vinny was a professional boxer and a guy with an incredible can-do attitude. At only five feet seven inches, he packed a powerful punch due to years of extreme training. He made his professional debut in 1983 and by 1987 was the IBF World Lightweight Champion.

He moved around in different weight classes over the next several years and fought (and lost) in title bouts to the likes of Roger Mayweather and Hector "Macho" Camacho.

After settling in at the junior middleweight division, he was flying high on October 1, 1991, when he won the WBA World Junior Middleweight Championship. Vinny's rise was fascinating and improbable up to that point, but it pales in comparison with the rest of his story.

Just a few weeks after regaining the championship, Vinny was sitting in the passenger seat of a friend's car when they crashed head-on with a car that had crossed over into their lane. He was fortunate to escape with his life. When he awoke in the hospital, Vinny learned that his neck was broken in several locations. All the doctors agreed it was unlikely he would ever walk again, and of course it was a certainty that his career as a professional fighter was over.

But he refused to give up. He made it clear that if he couldn't fight, he didn't want to live. Everyone around him advised him to give up his dream, and presumed that over time, he would. But Paz saw it as a life-and-death decision, so this was the leverage he used on himself.

First, he blew everyone away when he got up out of his wheelchair. And, true to his word, he defied his doctors' orders and started working out within weeks after being released from the hospital. He did this despite the fact he had to wear a neck brace called a halo, a heavy circular device made of metal that was screwed through his scalp and into his skull with four bolts. The doctor ordered him to wear this 24/7 for three months, but that didn't stop him from his workout regimen!

Whenever I'm out for a run and hit a wall and start to think about turning around and going home,

I picture Vinny lifting weights with that medieval torture device embedded in his head, and the image pushes me forward.

Believe it or not, Paz was back in the ring just 13 months after the accident! And he didn't just show up to be a punching bag; on the night of his comeback, he soundly beat his opponent, Luis Santana.

Before his retirement from the ring in 2004, he won and lost various titles, (including beating Roberto Duran two times) and ended his career with a 50–10 record. Think about it – after breaking his neck, he fought professionally for another 13 years!

To my mind, this man, affectionately known as the Pazmanian Devil, is the epitome of the power of determination, courage, and willingness to trust one's own instincts. But don't take my word for it; if you want to be truly inspired, watch *Bleed for This*, the feature film based on Vinnie's life.

Profit from your mistakes
*A man must be big enough to admit his mistakes,
smart enough to profit from them,
and strong enough to correct them.*
John C. Maxwell

When the Going Gets Tough—And It Will!

To quote the great Sam Cooke, "Mama said there'll be days like this," and you can bet that when you sign on for a *Go 4 It!* life, you will encounter times when you will want to pack it in because of a mistake you made. That's the time to access all of your resources, lick your wounds, and honestly assess what went wrong and why.

The title of one of my favorite John Maxwell books says it all: *Sometimes You Win, Sometimes You Learn.* When you make a mistake, record the details in your notebook so you will have it straight for future reference. Let's say you trusted someone who later proved untrustworthy. Honestly evaluate why you were so gullible, and protect yourself from making that error again.

Your personal board of advisers

Now that you have identified the goals you want to reach, you will naturally start to notice that there are people all around you who already have found success in the areas you chose. Let's say you would like to start a business. Talk with people who are successful entrepreneurs, and show up with your notebook and a list of questions, so you will remember their advice. Or perhaps you know someone who transformed their physique; ask them how they did it. The world is filled with helpful, generous people, who usually want to share their knowledge.

Start by writing down the names of a few people you would like to work with as your mentor, and make a commitment to reach out to at least one person per week. If possible, try to do something for them in advance, but at the very least, be certain to repay the favor in some way after someone has helped you.

I know that this might sound a bit scary, but try it a few times and you will see that it works. In general, do not be afraid to ask for help. What have you got to lose? Remember, if you don't A-S-K, you won't G-E-T.

Keep in mind that you are not in this alone, so it's important to develop your network. I'm not talking about just being Facebook friends or growing your LinkedIn circle; I want you to take real action. Join a church or temple, check in at the local Chamber of Commerce, or volunteer your time in your community. Sign up at Meetup.com, and find others who have shared interests and goals.

Always be learning

Read, watch, listen, and learn all the time! Feed your brain with inspirational thoughts and images. Carry your notebook with you so you will always be prepared to jot down the valuable pieces of information you hear, such as a quote, a book or a movie someone recommends, or a lead on a great teacher in your area.

In this day and age, there is obviously a wealth of free information online. Please check out my website at **RobertPascuzzi.com**, where you will find inspirational videos you can subscribe for free for (Energizers), my blog, and links to many of my favorite teachers.

Perseverance is the hallmark of the achiever. When it all comes down to it, I see it as the single most important trait. The best-laid plans will run into roadblocks and setbacks during the execution phase, but perseverance is what will carry you through to the other side.

There are countless examples of great leaders who have made a significant contribution to mankind but made magnificent blunders along the way. Consider Steve Jobs. He was literally fired from the company he founded, spent years as an outcast from Apple, and then returned to transform it into one of the most successful companies in the world! If Steve Jobs can learn by his mistakes, then perhaps you and I can allow ourselves to fail and learn as well.

To persevere is to overcome the self-doubts, fears, challenges and doubters or detractors you encounter. When you persevere, even on a small scale, you are teaching your brain that you can do it, that you have what it takes to get it done, to become the person you set out to become.

And *that* will make you powerful!

CHAPTER 10
Faith and the Law of Attraction

Nothing is impossible.
The word itself says "I'm possible!"
Audrey Hepburn

You'll recall that in the second chapter you made a Definite Decision and committed that decision to writing and dated it. In so doing, you made a covenant with yourself. For those readers who were serious about that promise, it might have been a little frightening yet exciting, while for others it seemed silly, perhaps some nonsensical hocus-pocus. Those folks – the cynics, doubters, skeptics, and naysayers – might even have turned tail and run at the first sight of a brick wall in the distance.

But if you have read this far and followed through with the exercises, then you have started to discover that there are techniques for hopping over the wall, avoiding it entirely, or forming a team and crashing through!

It's particularly good news for you gung-ho readers who are still here and want to learn more about how to *Go 4 It!*, because this chapter is dealing with information that is known to millions but rarely applied correctly. It's used incorrectly is because the very concept seems fantastic and unbelievable, despite the fact that we see daily proof of its existence. You have doubtless heard of this principle: It's called the Law of Attraction.

> *Whatever the mind can conceive*
> *and believe, it can achieve.*
> *Napoleon Hill*

The basic idea behind the Law of Attraction is that the universe is controlled by an infinite intelligence that operates in and connects all of us, and that our thoughts can attract positive or negative people and experiences. While there have been numerous recent bestselling books that teach and explore this idea, if you are interested in learning more, I recommend that you read the granddaddy of all books on The Law of Attraction, *Think and Grow Rich*, by Napoleon Hill.

Unfortunately, the Law of Attraction has gotten something of a bad rap in the recent past, because it has been misunderstood; some would say it's because it has been misrepresented in certain circles. One thing is for certain – when you truly understand its depths, it is a powerful weapon that should definitely be in your arsenal.

If you have read some of the recent books or watched some online videos that promote the Law of Attraction, you may be under the impression that great things will happen simply by changing your attitude. Turn off the negative switch and turn on the positive switch.

Changing your attitude is definitely a primary key, but as the "risk management team" in your head has already asserted, a true and lasting change in attitude takes a deeper understanding of how paradigms exist in your head and how new paradigms can be planted, nurtured and grown. Tools I've shared with you such as positive affirmations, and journaling and envisioning the end result are significant techniques that will encourage and nurture those new, powerful positive paradigms.

These processes, however, must always be accompanied by a clear action plan. As you have doubtless figured out by now, decisive action is the essence of the *Go 4 It!* program. When I had all those invoices buried at the back of my desk, I know it was the action I took – writing out checks for all of the invoices as if the money was there and the bills could be paid – that offered the confident kind of energy that began to attract changes in my life to actually create this end result.

You must act on your dream, even if you're not sure of all the steps between where you stand now and the end result you seek.

I'd like to return for a moment to the aspect of negative thoughts and negative affirmations. At some level, we all know that thinking and speaking negatively isn't going to bring us what we want. So, who in their right mind would repeat negative affirmations? The answer is: all of us. Even if we don't put voice to it, when we allow our thoughts to be preoccupied with projections of failure and doubt, that eventual reality is going to come hurtling down the rails of our lives.

Faith and the Law of Attraction

Worrying is like praying for what you don't want.
Anonymous

Part of our human condition is that we are always living in a state of uncertainty, because we are obviously not capable of knowing what is going to happen tomorrow. Those of us who choose to worry and project problems are very likely to get more of the same. When we choose to be thankful each day, we are likely to attract positive experiences.

I can simplify this further by pointing out that the Law of Attraction is really another way of stating the Golden Rule: Do unto others as you would have others do unto you.

This law is more than just a sensible theory – it makes your life more pleasurable and also causes you to be more successful in business. In the society we live in presently, where "greed is good" and "what's mine is mine," this simple Golden Rule may seem like a quaint idea, but I see its power in action every day.

People often ask me why our company, Creative Planning, has become the number one wealth management firm in America. Of course, there are a multitude of reasons for the success of any company (beginning with an attitude of excellence supported by a staff committed to the same goal), but I believe our commitment to always place the customer's interests above our own is the secret to our success.

You might ask why I would be willing to give away such a valuable secret, and the answer is simple: because the unfortunate truth is that the financial services industry thrives on practices that generally place the interests of the company ahead of those of the customer. I know it will take a massive cultural shift for most of our competitors to change.

The Seven Day experiment

Here's something to try: As you go about your daily interactions, make a point of placing the interests of others above your own. This may look as if you are losing out in short run, but I assure you that will not be the case. Let the other fellow zip ahead of you as you are merging. Give up your seat on the bus. Greet a stranger with a smile. Give a colleague or a client the benefit of the doubt, even if you know he or she has made a mistake. Actually listen to your friend instead of interrupting. Share your wealth (even if you have very little), with others.

Give this a try for a week and keep track of events in your journal. Then, review the entries after seven days. I guarantee that you will feel better about yourself, and moreover, you will recognize the boomerang effect of goodwill.

> *Did I offer peace today? Did I bring a smile to*
> *someone's face? Did I say words of healing?*
> *Did I let go of my anger and resentment?*
> *Did I forgive? Did I love?*
> *These are the real questions.*
> Henri Nouwen

Try a little gratitude

I find that it's much too easy to lose sight of what's really important to us as we get wrapped up in our daily business and are confronted with the petty annoyances and disappointments that are bound to occur. Face it, folks, other people just will not always do what we want them to do. Whether it's the teller at the bank, your children or significant other, a boss who never sees eye-to-eye with you, or the investor you were counting on to back your business who changes his mind at the last minute.

Yep, we all know that some people will disappoint us, and, of course, we will disappoint others. The key is to develop a mindset that will stop you from spiraling down into self-pity and doubt. The absolute best antidote for is gratitude. As Tony Robbins says, "When you are grateful, fear disappears and abundance appears." Of course, that's easier said than done when things do not seem to be going your way for a prolonged period of time.

It's important that you understand, though, that gratitude has everything to getting in the right frequency with The Law of Attraction. In fact, most mentors will tell you that is THE main thing. A mind bathed in gratitude simply cannot reach out in a negative way.

There is a simple, proven technique for combating those negative emotions. It's called a Gratitude List, and I learned about it from a friend who has been attending AA meetings for a long time. When he told me about the concept, I had my doubts, (because it was just too simple), but he was so convincing that I decided to give it a try.

That was around 14 years ago, and today I

still have that that original piece of paper in a safe place. It's a bit tattered now, but I treasure it and consider it a living document. Whenever I feel that my mind is starting to take a wrong turn, I fish it out, read it from start to finish, and frequently add to it. I keep it in order to remind myself of all of the gifts I have been given in my life, and I suggest you do the same.

I've left a few spaces below as an encouragement to you to get started on your list. Mine begins with my family, my faith in God, my work, my friends, and even my ability to walk, talk, see, hear, taste, and so on. Write down whatever comes to mind for you and be as specific as possible. Everyone you love should be on the list. Every blessing you've been given deserves mention. It's impossible to make a mistake here, because even those people with whom you have conflict (an in-law or a co-worker, perhaps?) is part of your universe and exists in your world to teach you some lesson you may need to learn. I suggest that you strike while the iron is hot and start the list below, but then get a large piece of paper so you can add to it in the years to come.

Go 4 It!

GRATITUDE LIST

Izzy

My FAMILY

My FRIENDS

My HEALTH

My WEALTH

My HOUSE

My CAR

My WORK/CAREER

My SIGHT

My HEARING

My ABILITY TO WALK/RUN

My TALENT

My FAITH

ALL THE KNOWLEDGE AND WISDOM
THAT I HAVE, AND CONTINUE, TO
RECEIVE.

144

Faith and the Law of Attraction

Faith and our abundant universe

I've mentioned that I wasn't born with a natural go-for-it personality, and my observations tell me that most people fall into the same category. This is most evident when I am conducting seminars and watch as people go through the processes and eventually reach the moment when they are ready to commit to taking a leap into the unknown.

Fortunately, the majority of people sitting in the room who decided to attend a seminar with a title like *Go 4 It!* are usually able to overcome their initial barriers, but when it comes to actually pulling the trigger, a certain percentage will come smack up against their greatest challenge: A lack of faith.

Without faith, it is very difficult to achieve our goals. As I discussed in the last chapter, regardless of how carefully we plan or the amount of effort we exert, barriers will be tossed in our path and problems will arise on a regular basis. It's at those times that we will be tempted to crawl back into that safe and secure comfort zone of our own making. I guarantee there will come a time when the only thing that will allow you to soldier on will be your faith, so it's important to learn how to tap into the form of faith that

145

works for you.

Toward the end of the day at my live events, we finally arrive at the point when each person is asked to stand up and share his or her intentions with the group. The only condition is that everyone must be utterly and completely honest. This is the *Go 4 It!* moment of truth.

Most of the people are chomping at the bit to get out the door and jump into their new challenges, but there will also be a few who resist, despite the fact that they are excited about their plan, know exactly what they want to do, and even intellectually comprehend that they must do it. But, because the pathway looks murky and all the answers are not yet known, they remain undecided. Usually a group discussion ensues, and they will be assured that all the evidence points to their Definite Decision dramatically improving their lives, and that they now have all the tools necessary for success. Usually the doubters will come to their own conclusion: They simply lack faith.

This is a tough subject for many people because it is often confused with religious faith. If one has faith in God or a Creator, that's an advantage in my opinion, but my purpose is to try to help others develop faith in the abundance of the universe and to recognize that they live their everyday lives completely dependent upon a universe that functions to support us – if we know how to ASK, we will GET.

At this juncture I'll usually pose a rhetorical question such as: "Well, have you ever been on a jet plane?

"When you boarded, did you know for certain that the engines were in working order, and that birds wouldn't fly into them (after all, that did happen to a jet Sully Sullenberger was piloting). Are you certain some other lethal incident isn't about to happen at 35,000 feet?"

"Well, no."

"But you got on the plane anyway. So you must have had faith in the plane and the pilot and the birds."

And the discussion ensues from there. This process is convincing to some, but for others, the very last step of developing faith is just a bridge too far, and fear wins out.

I hope that in your case, you choose to live life in a spirit of hope and optimism, because if we are confident and honestly contribute our part, the universe will provide.

In my case, I do believe in God, and in times of turmoil, I will turn to my Creator and ask for help and guidance. As you might have figured out by now, I like to manage things and be at the helm, so I frequently need to remind myself to stop, and find a quiet place to bow my head.

I would like to end this section by sharing a quote from John Earl Shoaff, who is little known today but had a tremendous influence on some of our most important contemporary inspirational teachers. I've read this hundreds of times, yet it still has the power to reawaken my understanding of the abundance of the universe every time I read it.

Life never, never withholds anything from anyone. Love, health, wealth, companionship. All these exist in infinite abundance. We alone are the ones that prevent our own good from flowing, simply because we are not aware of nature's abundance and the tremendous power dormant in each of us.

My story of gratitude
> *It doesn't matter where you are. You are nowhere compared to where you can go.*
> Bob Proctor

Shortly before I started my campaign to participate in the Ironman Triathlon, I decided to leave the big national insurance company for whom I was selling, in order to start my own business managing 401K programs for small to mid-sized companies. I had many frustrations at the large firm, but my major complaint was that I was permitted to sell only the products the company represented. With my own company, on the other hand, I would have the freedom to make certain that the programs I recommended would suit each client's particular needs, even if it generated less profit for me.

While the concept of 401K plans is well known now, I began my business when companies were first transitioning out of fully sponsored pension plans, and I could sense this was the wave of the future. At that time the average employee was usually confused by the concept, particularly those who were accustomed to company-sponsored pension plans.

While still employed at the insurance firm, I began to get involved with retirement programs and it soon became apparent to me that I loved the idea of helping folks plan for their future. I also discovered that I would come alive when I had the opportunity to talk to groups about the importance of saving for retirement, tax advantages that could be theirs, the principles of money, and why a 401K plan benefits both the company and the employees. I knew that I was helping people secure their financial futures and loved to explain the intricacies of the investment product in a simplified manner that was clear and understandable.

I had found my passion at last! Other people may be able to stand at center stage and belt out an aria or play a mean guitar, but my gift is retirement planning, and I am so grateful I found it. It may not sound sexy, but I still get a charge when I show someone how they can create a retirement fund worth half a million dollars by starting early and simply contributing $100 per week. I derive a great deal of satisfaction from knowing that I have now helped thousands of individuals prepare for a secure future.

By this time in my life, I had developed my *Go 4 It!* chops, and so I knew with certainty that leaving the security of a big firm and starting a new business in an emerging field was the right thing to do. Once I made my Definite Decision to start the company, I put aside the cash reserves I would need to support my family and the new venture until the cash started to flow in the right direction. My immediate need was to find an inexpensive office space, and it was in this seemingly insignificant act that my entire future turned.

We never know when our lives are going to be transformed by opportunities that will be placed in our hands. This is true in all aspects of life, including love relationships, business and spiritual matters. As with my choice of office space, an event might seem insignificant at the moment, or appear to be mere happenstance. That was the case the night I went to a club with a friend and wound up meeting Kelly. From that moment on, our lives were transformed. I know she was a gift from God to me. I certainly wasn't in control that night, but the abundant universe provided nonetheless.

Neither was it in my control the day that I happened to run into a friend who mentioned that Peter Mallouk, a mutual acquaintance, might have some space available at his firm, Creative Planning. Today I consider Peter my closest friend, and a great mentor, but at the time I hardly knew him.

Peter had recently purchased Creative Planning, and the entire staff consisted of something in the area of five or six employees. He had a cubicle with a phone on the desk that he rented to me for what I recall was a very reasonable fee. Thirteen years later, we number more than 400 employees, and Peter just broke ground to start work on a massive new building to manage our growth.

Peter, the President and Chief Investment Officer of Creative Planning, is simply one of the smartest and most generous people I have ever met. He just naturally embodies an attitude of abundance, which I think accounts for his extraordinary abilities, and particularly for his decisiveness. When Peter makes a decision to do something, he does it now. He doesn't wait for tomorrow.

But the reality is that "Bob's 401K business" didn't take off until Peter and I figured out that we could leverage his connections and accounts and my cold-calling ability. During that time, I got to spend a great deal of windshield time with Peter, and our friendship grew. I had the opportunity to observe his work habits and fearlessness. He also operates at a very high level of integrity, as I learned on one of our very first sales calls together.

One day I managed to cold-call our way into a

meeting with a company that had a $100 million re-
tirement plan. At that time Creative Planning managed about that much money overall, so naturally we
were concerned that they might ask about the size of
our business. We decided to give it our best shot.

I was sweating bullets when we got into the
packed boardroom and, of course, it wasn't long
before someone popped the obvious question about
how much money we managed. I just looked over at
Peter, and he said, "Well, about the same amount that
you have in your retirement plan." Needless to say,
we were soon ushered out the door.

The point is that Peter didn't try to fudge the answer. We only had one option, and that was to tell the
truth. So, the first few years were sort of like watching grass grow. We were making progress, but it was
almost impossible to see.

Of course, there were days when I was discouraged, but I believed in our mission, and in the simple
concept of always putting the client first. Whatever
your business, I advise you to embrace this concept.
At Creative Planning, it's not enough that we charge
the lowest fees (which we do); we place our clients'
interests above our own. By hiring experts who know

every detail of their business, we make fully informed decisions, and therefore can be completely transparent.

After several years of very hard work, people on the outside suddenly noticed Creative Planning and began calling it an "overnight success!" We were named to Barron's Top 100 list. Initially, when we came in at number 19, we suddenly had a much more interesting story to tell. It wasn't long before other publications and financial media outlets began to take notice, and we made other "best of" lists. This helped motivate us, and we climbed up the Barron's list the next year at number 4. We only climbed higher on Barron's list from there. Today we are managing more than $37 billion, and just in my division alone, in retirement plans, we manage more than $2 billion.

The Law of Attraction functions in all aspects of our lives, and particularly in the world of business. If you continually do the right thing by placing your customer's interests above your own. This is true whether you are running a nationally known wealth management firm or a neighborhood dry cleaner – your clients will tell others, and people will come knocking at your door.

Faith and the Law of Attraction

One of the more surprising people to turn up at our door was Tony Robbins.

I've mentioned here many of the inspirational teachers I have studied over the years, but Tony Robbins has unquestionably had a great impact on my life. Almost 25 years ago, I scraped together the money to attend a Tony Robbins event in Chicago called *Unleash the Power Within*. I'd listened to his tapes and read his books, but there is really nothing like one of his live events.

I remember I returned home after that weekend and announced to Kelly that I had a goal: One day I would personally get to know Tony. I'm sure she kindly reassured me, not taking me very seriously. But, that day has arrived, because Tony is now on our board of directors and holds the title of Chief of Investor Psychology.

The story of how Tony Robbins came to Creative Planning demonstrates exactly how the law of attraction operates. Unbeknownst to anyone at Creative Planning, Tony decided to search out the firms that were truly putting clients' interests first His search led him to our company. Though this might appear to be a case of simply being "at the right place at the right time," in fact it was the result of years of effort, determination and perseverance. In other words, it didn't just happen by accident, it was intentional!

Of course, for me personally, this has been a tremendously gratifying experience.

I believe that our lives are filled with moments of grace. Some will fly past almost unnoticed, but others are electric and will be seared into your mind the instant they occur. The day I walked into Peter's office to meet Tony definitely falls into the latter category.

Tony is a big presence, a genuine force of nature, and I knew that something in my life instantly clicked into place and came full circle as soon as I grasped his hand. I showed Tony my well-worn goal book, and in his typically effusive and generous manner he told me how impressed he was that I had followed through and done the work. After chatting for a bit, we got down to discussing business. The room grew quiet, and I took the opportunity to say what was in my heart.

"I just want you to know that ... you have been one of the most influential individuals in my life, even though we never met until today. You've had a significant impact on me." Then I looked over at Peter.

Faith and the Law of Attraction

"There are two people besides my Dad who have impacted me the most; and I'm sitting in the room with both of them right now. This is a very special moment for me."

Whatever we are waiting for – peace of mind, contentment, grace, the inner awareness of simple abundance – it will surely come to us, but only when we are ready to receive it with an open and grateful heart.
Sarah Ban Breathnach

CHAPTER 11
Now Is the Time

If you wait too long for the perfect moment,
the perfect moment will pass you by.
Wisdom found in a fortune cookie

As you can see, there are just a few pages remaining, and you know what that means – the moment to take action has arrived! This is when you finally toss out your old excuses and replace them with complete and utter honesty. You might remember that I began my *Go 4 It!* journey many years ago. I took a deep and sincere look in the mirror and was shaken to the core when I discovered that I was about to sleepwalk through a life of mediocrity. Fortunately, I was given the gift of clarity, for which I will be forever grateful. I hope that by sharing my experience, I have repaid that debt in some small measure.

As I stated at the beginning of the book, it was my intention to show you exactly how to make a dramatic transformation in your life, and to do so in the space of a few hours. My goal was to simplify the message so that you could begin on your journey without delay. I sincerely hope that you will start today and continue to use these techniques in the future as you seek your destiny.

At the outset, it is of absolute importance that you firmly imbed the end result you seek for your life as THE Force that motivates you. Along the way, always remember to help others and live with integrity.

As the stories of such people as Jonathan Goldsmith, Nelson Mandela, Dwayne "The Rock" Johnson, and Vinny Paz demonstrate (see these and the other inspiring *Go 4 It!* profiles that follow), there will be times when our desires will be confronted by challenges, and these will only be overcome by a combination of courage, confidence and determination. That's when you will discover the defining difference between wanting to do something and having to do it.

Sometimes you need to have your back slammed

against the wall in order to throw down the gaunt-let and stop messing around with your life. When you are certain – when you convert "might do" into "MUST do"– this is when you will exert the lever-age on yourself to push through with incontrovert-ible ferocity.

Make no mistake about it, in order to get to this point, you will need to find your fuel, and by that I mean whatever is unique to you that will compel you toward excellence. The good news is that once you truly own your fuel, you will become accustomed to stepping over the barriers that are just a part of living a *Go 4 It!* life.

I'm not going to wish you good luck on your jour-ney, because I'm convinced the universe will provide for you as long as you do your part and seize the op-portunities that are presented every single day. So, live with an expectation of abundance and always be on the lookout for good things to fall into your lap. Universe doesn't know how to let you down. You are always supported, so lean on that support.

When you made your Definite Decision and signed and dated it, you identified the dream that is unique to you, and made a commitment to transform it into reality. Follow through. Take that commitment seriously. And you will discover that success awaits you. It is just a matter of time, effort and faith. Believe that anything is possible, because it is.

CHAPTER 12

Inspiring *Go 4 It!* Profiles

There are many people who have inspired, influenced, taught, and guided me over the years, but I had to pick just a few to include in this book. The following people represent some of the best of the best, in my opinion. They always *Go 4 It!*, they never quit, they didn't throw themselves a pity party when things weren't going well, and they didn't sit back and become complacent when things were going well. I hope these profiles will be as inspiring for you as they have been for me.

Jonathan Goldsmith

*The best time to go for broke is when
you're already there.*

Jonathan Goldsmith is an actor with more than 350 stage, film, and TV credits, but he is best known as The Most Interesting Man in the World. His long-standing stint with Dos Equis increased the beer's sales more than 15 percent; he appeared on billboards, print ads, and TV commercials for ten years, and became an internationally beloved figure.

At his audition, Goldsmith was asked to improvise and end with the line "... and that's how I arm-wrestled Fidel Castro." For thirty dazzling minutes the casting directors were treated to highlights from The Most Interesting Man's past adventures as Goldsmith freely ad-libbed, channeling his friend and sailing partner, the late Fernando Lamas.

Jonathan had to hold on to his dreams and hopes through many long years of get-up-and-go—working on his craft, fighting for recognition, overcoming personal hardship. He knows well that in real life, being interesting is not just a part you play, it's an ongoing learning process. Goldsmith remains interesting, to say the least, as a businessman, theater teacher, sailboat enthusiast, and memoirist, and supports several charitable causes. After being replaced in the Dos Equis ads by French actor Augustin Legrand, he was quickly taken up by Astral Tequila. He also serves as editor emeritus for True.Ink, a website that "celebrates The Noble Pursuit, a mix of adventure, expertise, and kindness," where he creates its True Master columns on how to celebrate a life well lived.

In an article for Politico.com, Goldsmith wrote, "I can say with certainty that to be interesting, you have to be interested. You can watch the parade that is life—and live vicariously through others, as many do—or you can get in and participate in your own journey. And the best time to go for broke is when you're already there."

J. K. Rowling

We carry all the power we need inside ...
We have the power to imagine better.

J. K. Rowling penned her first book, *Rabbit*, at the age of six, her first novel, about cursed diamonds, at eleven, and cemented her passion for writing studying French and Classics at Exeter University. While waiting for a delayed train, she got the idea for a book series, and for five years she mapped it out, even while living in Portugal, teaching English, and marrying. When the marriage failed, she returned to live in Edinburgh with the first three chapters of the first book, her six-month-old daughter, and the determination to "direct all my energy into finishing the only work that mattered to me." As a single mom, money was so tight she needed assistance, yet her persistence was awarded with "the best letter I'd ever received." Bloomsbury Children's Books would publish her book and give her a 2,500-pound advance. Still, her editor warned, "royalties might not amount to much." Rowling has become the first author to earn 1 billion dollars solely from her writing (with profits from the Potter book series and its eight movies, adult books, and her first screenplay, for *Fantastic Beasts and Where to Find Them*. She has remarried, has two other children, and dedicates a sizable portion of her wealth to two charitable trusts. She continues to write books, stage plays, screenplays, and her 2008 Harvard Commencement address became a bestseller. While her most famous storybook character does indeed employ magic, Rowling doesn't think it's necessary. "We carry all the power we need inside ... we have the power to *imagine better.*"

Muhammad Ali

I don't have to be who you want me to be;
I'm free to be who I want.

Cassius Clay Jr. was thirteen years old when Emmett Till, who was only one year older than he, was lynched in Mississippi. Clay was shattered by the event. It was the first of many confrontations with racial injustice that he would witness over his lifetime, and he was furious.

Joe Martin, a white policeman who owned a local gym, urged Clay to channel his anger into learning how to box properly. He was soon impressed by the young man's natural talents and urged him to "gamble your life" at the 1960 Olympics in Rome. Clay gambled and returned with the gold—and the ticket to a professional boxing career. He was eighteen.

Four years later, he dethroned Sonny Liston for the heavyweight title, one of three he won during a career total of 56–5, and changed his name to Muhammad Ali to declare his rejection of white domination during the Civil Rights Movement.

Muhammad Ali had been everyone's favorite boxer when he was Cassius Clay, but when he refused to be drafted into the United States Army in 1967, he was brutalized in the press and his reputation took more of a knocking than he ever did in the ring. His refusal to take part in the Vietnam conflict cost him millions of dollars, three years of exile from the ring, and the loss of his titles. He was convicted of draft evasion but awarded conscientious-objector status on appeal by the Supreme Court in 1971, which enabled him to resume boxing. He could have rested on his Olympic gold and previous wins, but he came back swinging and won not only heavyweight bouts, but the hearts of sports fans everywhere as a man who was willing to risk everything for what he believed was right.

Ali embraced the Black Muslim faith and later orthodox Islam, became the first boxer to appear on a box of Wheaties, and received the Medal of Freedom from President George W. Bush in 2005. He lit the Olympic cauldron in Atlanta in 1996 with trembling hands that evidenced his long battle with Parkinson's disease. Throughout his life, he was mocked relentlessly by the press and the public, but he never gave in. He said, "I don't have to be who you want me to be; I'm free to be who I want."

Nelson (Rolihlahla) Mandela

It always seems impossible until it's done.

As a twelve-year-old-ward of the royal family of the royal Thembu people, Mandela absorbed the elders' stories of valor, and dreamed of making his own contribution to his people in a country racially divided. The ruling white Afrikaaners had created a system of institutionalized racial segregation and discrimination strictly enforced in South Africa, often with violence. Mandela joined the African National Congress (ANC) in 1944 and fought against injustice, only to be tried and convicted multiple times for civil disobedience.

Even while imprisoned, he nonetheless kept working to help the ANC negotiate the end of apartheid. He was finally released, after twenty-seven years, by then-president F. W. de Klerk in 1990, largely because of growing international pressure. Mandela became president of the ANC in 1991, succeeding Oliver Tambo, his partner in Mandela & Tambo, the country's first black law firm, which they founded in 1952.

Terrible riots broke out after his release, but de

Klerk and Mandela worked together to end apartheid officially, and the two were awarded the Nobel Peace Prize in 1993. In 1994, Mandela voted for the first time, and in a multiracial general election, the National Assembly elected him the country's first black president. His inauguration May 10, 1994, was televised globally to more than 1 billion viewers. Serving just one five-year term, he devoted the rest of his life to combating poverty and HIV/AIDS until he died at age 95 in 2013. How did he keep pursuing equality for blacks and whites in South Africa for nearly five decades. As Mandela said, "It always seems impossible until it's done."

Colonel Sanders

No hours, nor amount of labor,
nor amount of money would deter me
from giving the best that
there was in me.

Col. Harland Sanders, the icon of the fast-food franchise he created, KFC (Kentucky Fried Chicken), was born in 1890. He was just shy of thirteen when he left school to pursue jobs on the farm and off; he worked for the railroad, served a brief stint serving the army in Cuba while underage, studied law, and sold insurance. The first steady success he had was a service station/motel/café he owned in Corbin, Kentucky. "I made a resolve then that I was going to amount to something if I could. And no hours, nor amount of labor, nor amount of money would deter me from giving the best that there was in me." That *Go 4 It!* attitude served him well until the rerouting of the interstate highway collapsed his business, leaving him only his $105 Social Security check for income. At an age when most men retire, he said, "It wasn't a matter of giving up, just a problem of what to do next." One thing he did know was how to make "finger lickin' good " fried chicken, which he sold door-to-door. In 1956, he arranged his first franchise, and by 1960, he had 400 outlets. Those grew to 900 in the US, Canada, England, and Japan in 1964, when he was offered $2 million to sell his US portion. His contract assured him he'd remain the company spokesperson, always in his signature white suit and bolo tie. He died in 1980, at age 90, with a personal worth of $3.5 million. The company he began? Billions earned.

Lillian Vernon

> *I never gave up, and I never let anyone*
> *get in my way.*

Lillian Vernon, like many postwar women, left her studies at New York University to marry. The former Lilli Menasche of Leipzig, Germany, whose family had fled Nazi Germany in the 1930s, was first married to Sam Hochberg, whose family owned a store in Mount Vernon, New York. She anglicized her first name, co-opted her in-laws' business home, and gave birth to Lillian Vernon.

She was pregnant, twenty-four years old, and worried about survival. She decided to risk $2,000 of their wedding money, and, in 1951, advertised a personalized leather handbag, at $2.99, with matching belt, at $1.99, in Seventeen magazine and garnered $32,000 in orders. Her first catalog debuted in 1956; the company incorporated in 1965 and had its first million-dollar sales year in 1970. That initial effort begun at her kitchen table, and segued into nine catalogs, fifteen outlet stores, two websites, a business-to-business division, and an annual gross income of $300 million.

She had created an entirely new retail market: the

themed catalog with products unavailable anywhere else, and her signature service, free monograms. Using her "golden gut" to decide what products to buy, she was the first to create seasonal catalogs for Easter and Halloween and the first to offer the gift-with-purchase. She sold the business in 2003 for $60.5 million to Ripplewood Holdings, Overcoming obstacles from skeptical male lenders at banks and defying criticisms for working mothers, Lillian Vernon became, in 1987, the first woman-owned company to be listed on the American Stock Exchange.

Ms. Vernon, who died in 2015 at age eighty-eight, said, "I never gave up, and I never let anyone get in my way."

Duane Douglas Johnson "The Rock"
What do I want? I want the world.

What do you think of when you think of a rock? Perhaps the eons of pressure and cycles of heat and cooling that went into forming it. Maybe you think of toughness, strength, endurance.

Now what do you think of when you think of The Rock, Dwayne Johnson? With his dazzling smile, arresting good looks, and impressive skill set, maybe you think that everything just comes naturally to him, that he probably didn't have to work all that hard to get where he is … but The Rock was formed by pressures and cycles, by terrifying ups and downs, blessings and losses, just as stone is carved by wind, water, and heat.

Dwayne Douglas Johnson was born in California in May 1972, an only child. His father, Rocky, was a professional wrestler who made a precarious living on the circuit, and the family moved frequently. When Dwayne was only fourteen, he faced his first *Go 4 It!* challenge. He and his mother were living in Hawaii while his father was on tour, and had been struggling for a long time. The car had been repossessed, Dwayne was involved with a criminal element in Waikiki, and one day he came home to see an eviction notice and a padlock on the door.

"We were living in an efficiency that cost $120 a week ... My mom starts bawling ... 'Where are we going to live? What are we going to do?'" While she looked for work, The Rock—young as he was—realized he had to do something to change his life. "That was the tipping point," he says. "It was about, 'What can I control with these two hands?' The only thing I could do was train and build my body."

He went to work, bodybuilding and training, up at dawn, relentlessly driving himself to do better and get stronger. His talent and dedication brought him a full football scholarship at the University of Miami, and a rare chance to play in his freshman year. He was on top of the world when he sustained a severe injury to his shoulder, followed by a deep depression. Five lackluster years followed, until he was cut from the Canadian Football League's Calgary Stampeders.

The Rock returned to Miami and called his father for a ride to Tampa with about seven dollars in his pocket. This was another low point, and again he fought his way out of it, this time by training to become a WWF wrestler, winning seventeen championships, and becoming one of the most beloved "heels" (bad guys) in WWF history.

At the same time, he embarked on a film career and, without any acting training, went on to delight audiences with the *Fast Track* franchise, *Saturday Night Live* appearances, *The Scorpion King*, *The Mummy Returns*, and many other successful films. Anyone would think Johnson had reached the mountaintop. But, in 2010, he says, "It reached a point of, 'I'm not feeling authentic.'"

By this time, The Rock already knew he had it in him to get what he wanted. He went to work again, redefining himself and his goals. He took another hard look at his life and made the changes he needed to make. We'll be seeing a lot more of The Rock, who is said to have "the wit of **Willis**, the strength of **Schwarzenegger**, and the heart of **Stallone**." He is working on a second autobiography, following *The Rock Says* (2000) and is busy on numerous films, an HBO series (*Ballers*), a life coaching project (*Wake Up Call*), philanthropical efforts, and his family. There are even rumors he will run for president!

"I grew up where, when a door closed, a window didn't open," he says. "The only thing I had was cracks. I'd do everything to get through those cracks — scratch, claw, bite, push, bleed. Now the opportunity is here. The door is wide open and it's as big as a garage."

Malala Yousafzai

I don't want to be remembered as the girl who was shot. I want to be remembered as the girl who stood up.

It's difficult to erase the images surrounding the teenager shot in 2012 by the Taliban—not as an accidental casualty in the ongoing conflict in her home in Swat Valley, in Pakistan, but as a target for her work blogging (since the age of eleven) about the war and fighting for free quality education for girls in an area where the Taliban destroyed some 400 schools. When the Talib climbed into her school bus, he asked for Malala by name, then fired three shots at her, one lodged in her shoulder and one in her head. After four days in a Pakistani hospital, she was flown to England, placed in a medically induced coma, endured multiple surgeries, and therapy, yet fully recovered, and with no brain damage. She shows who she is, continuing her fight for education for girls around the world, pursuing her own education in England, where she now lives with her family. (Education is a family passion, and her father, Ziauddin, is an education advocate who once ran a school—as a toddler, Malala would wander in and imitate the teachers.)

For teaching that education for all is critical, Malala earned the 2014 Nobel Peace Prize, the youngest winner ever, at seventeen, sharing the honor with Indian children's rights activist Kailash Satyarthi. "Life is always dangerous. Some people get afraid of it. If they want to achieve their goal, they have to go [forward]. They have to move."

Vinny Paz, aka the Pazmanian Devil

It's easy to do if you're all in.

Vinny Paz was only the second boxer ever to hold world championships for both lightweight and junior middle lightweight titles when he was in an automobile accident that broke his neck and changed his life. Defying doctors' orders, lying to his parents, and sneaking out of the house to go train at the gym, he continued to box—wearing a halo brace drilled into his skull. His sparring partners were afraid they would reinjure him, but he persisted and won them over, training as hard as he ever had.

Thirteen months after his accident, Paz stepped back into the ring and beat Luis Santana in a ten-round decision that was considered the ultimate comeback battle in boxing history. He later won a twelve-round decision against the inimitable Roberto Duran.

Paz's career record is 50–10, including 30 KOs, five world titles in lightweight and middleweight categories, and the USBA title. He retired from the ring in 2004. In a BBC Sports report in 2016, Ben Dirs quotes Paz as saying, "The biggest lie in boxing is 'it's not that simple.' No one thought I would fight again but sometimes it's not as hard as people make it seem. So I was always going to give it one hell of a try. I just wasn't ready to call it quits.... Boxing gets in your blood and I didn't want to live if I wasn't able to do what I wanted to do."

Vinny Paz's amazing story of going for broke is told in the 2016 film *Bleed for This*, starring Miles Teller—check it out!

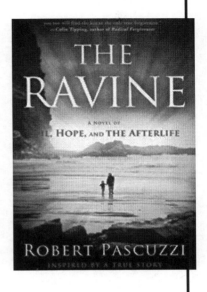

Made in the USA
San Bernardino, CA
20 December 2019